Best of Britain

Conal Gregory
and
Warren Knock

Cassell · Johnston and Bacon
London and Edinburgh

To our wives for their patience and understanding
while we compiled this guide.

First published 1975

© Conal Gregory and Warren Knock, 1975

Cassell & Collier Macmillan Publishers Ltd.
35 Red Lion Square, London WC1R 4SG
Tanfield House, Tanfield Lane , Edinburgh EH3 5LL and
at Sydney, Auckland, Toronto and Johannesburg
An Affiliate of Macmillan Inc., New York

ISBN 0 7179 2026 7 (paperback)

Printed in Great Britain by
Richard Clay (The Chaucer Press) Ltd.
Bungay, Suffolk

Contents

WESTERN ISLES

HIGHLAND

GRAMPIAN

TAYSIDE

CENTRAL ⑧

FIFE

STRATHCLYDE

LOTHIAN

BORDERS

DUMFRIES AND GALLOWAY

NORTHUMBERLAND

TYNE AND WEAR

CUMBRIA

DURHAM

CLEVELAND

ISLE OF MAN

NORTH YORKSHIRE ⑦

⑥ LANCASHIRE

WEST YORKSHIRE

HUMBERSIDE

MERSEYSIDE

GTR. MANCHESTER

SOUTH YORKSHIRE

GWYNEDD

CLWYD

CHESHIRE

DERBY

NOTTINGHAM

LINCOLN

SALOP

STAFFORD

⑨

LEICESTER

⑩ NORFOLK

POWYS

W. MIDLANDS

⑤

HEREFORD AND WORCESTER

WARWICK

NORTHAMPTON

⑪

BEDFORD

CAMBRIDGE

SUFFOLK

DYFED

WEST GLAMORGAN

MID GLAM.

GWENT

GLOUCESTER

OXFORD

BUCKINGHAM

HERTFORD

ESSEX

SOUTH GLAMORGAN

AVON

WILTSHIRE

BERKSHIRE

GT. LONDON ①

②

SOMERSET

HAMPSHIRE

SURREY

KENT

④

DORSET

WEST SUSSEX

EAST SUSSEX

DEVON

I. OF WIGHT

CORNWALL

① LONDON
② SOUTHERN ENGLAND
③ SOUTH WEST MIDLANDS
④ WEST COUNTRY
⑤ WALES AND THE BORDERS
⑥ NORTH WEST ENGLAND
⑦ YORKSHIRE AND THE NORTH EAST
⑧ SCOTLAND
⑨ THE MIDLANDS
⑩ EAST ANGLIA
⑪ HOME COUNTIES NORTH

Introduction

'What two ideas are more inseparable than Beer and Britannia?' asked Rev Sydney Smith (in his early 19th century *The Smiths of Smiths*). Today this has never been more so, with tourists rightly flocking to see the traditional English pub and with greater appreciation by the public of their pint.

Archaeologists are increasingly of the view that ale was first brewed in these islands in the Neolithic Period, over 5000 years ago. References to family brewing appear well before the Norman Conquest. It seems that the 17th-century proverb, thought to be referring to AD 1520, was somewhat out of date:

> Turkey, carps, hops, pickerel, and beer
> Came into England all in one year.

The history of beer and the alehouse in which it was drunk have been the subjects of enough studies, both in art—remembering William Hogarth's Beer Street—and in English literature, to make beer part of our national heritage.

Beer is the alcoholic liquor obtained by the fermentation of malt with hops. It is basically an uncomplicated drink: malted barley is ground, *mashed* with hot water to extract the malt from the heart of the barley and boiled with hops; yeast, which lives on the malt content and yields alcohol and carbon dioxide gas, is then introduced. The brewer's art is to control the quality of the ingredients and the fermenting process. This process takes approximately one week from the time of mashing until the beer is ready to be placed into the cask.

Good traditional beer depends on several factors. Firstly, it should be fermented from as pure a combination of malted barley and hops as possible, the proportion of hops to barley varying according to whether bitter, mild or some other type of beer is being produced. A recent trend towards the use of cheaper substitutes such as wheat flour, rice or potato starch should be discouraged, as these can give the beer a synthetic flavour. Of course, when beer is served chilled and in a fizzy state, it is much harder to appreciate its true character. If the use of substitute ingredients continues it may well be in the public interest for the Government to insist that beers made from less than 75 per cent pure malt are designated accordingly. A leaf could be taken out of the German law, still on the statute books and dating from the Middle Ages, prohibiting the use of rice, rice grits, flaked maize and other such items in the making of beer. It is, however, fair to say that a small proportion of flaked maize can help to give a beer body, and a number of brewers feel that it is a valuable ingredient.

Alcoholic content is a second factor in the making of good beer. For official purposes, such as the brewer's payment of duty, the strength of a beer is expressed as its Original Gravity (OG), which is calculated on the specific gravity of the wort (the liquid mixture of hops and malt before it is fermented including the dissolved natural sugar). Naturally the percentage of alcohol in the finished beer varies with its composition and how much it is fermented, but the OG is an indicator of the final alcoholic content. Thus an OG of 1038 would produce a beer with something like 3·8 per cent of alcohol by volume. Most British draught beers are between 2·5 (mild) and 4·5 (best bitter), with some barley wines or strong ales reaching 10 per cent. It is revealing that the national average OG of British beer has fallen from 1055 in 1900 through 1042·72 in 1923 and 1039·52 in 1933 to the 1973 level of 1036·99.

Increasingly the smaller breweries are publishing the OGs of their beers to show that they have not all followed this national trend to reduce the potential alcohol. On the other hand, legal compulsion to publish OG figures for all beers could result in drinkers choosing their beer on its strength alone, rather than by its flavour, or at least, assuming that the stronger beer is necessarily 'better'.

Traditional draught beer is generally regarded as quite different from container beer. With a natural ale the beer is racked straight into casks, some residual yeast remaining, and before the beer leaves the brewery some extra sugar and finings are added; the latter causes the sediment to fall to the bottom of the cask once the beer has arrived at the pub. In the meantime the fermentation will continue and the carbon dioxide gas naturally produced will give the final beer its traditional bubble. Container beers—including 'keg'—have their yeast cells filtered right out at the brewery and are often pasteurised, while carbon dioxide is frequently injected artificially to create a sparkle. The result is a clearer, more stable product than the traditional one, but it is dead and lacks the mellow fruity taste of natural 'live' ale and can even cause acidity in the stomach on account of its gassy nature.

It is difficult to keep traditional beer, for the publican needs a suitable cool cellar, skill in handling it owing to the residual sediment which is usually present in the cask and a hygienic approach to the way it is served. Traditional ale may be placed in the glass in one of three ways: gravity feed, where two holes are made in the cask, one for serving and the other for oxygen; casks where carbon dioxide is applied instead of oxygen to ensure that the beer can be drawn to the serving point (hence the expression 'top pressure'); thirdly, the beer engine in the form of a suction pump on the bar counter or a metered electric pump, which takes the work out of the suction-pulling gleaming beer engine handpumps; though usually your pint is served more quickly by handpump than by any other means.

The danger with the second of these three methods of serving traditional draught, by the system which pushes the beer to the bar by compressed air, is that the acceptable 4–5 lb per square inch pressure of carbon dioxide can be increased until the gas begins to get into the beer and alter its true character.

We have been speaking of beers in general, but what, in fact, are the main kinds of beer you will meet in a pub bar?

Bitter is generally a draught beer, yellow-golden in colour with a pronounced hop taste. The effect of making a bitter into 'keg' is often to give it a sweeter taste, and the colder temperature at which container beers are usually served obscures the real flavour. Most British beers (except lagers) are intended to be served at cellar temperature, cool, but not frosted. Brewers usually recommend 55 °F or thereabouts as ideal.

Mild ale, the weakest of draught beers, is made from darker malts and has a red-brown colour. It usually tends to be sweeter than bitter. There are some pale milds, weaker in alcohol but actually approaching bitter in flavour. A factor here is that fewer hops are used.

Strong ale is beer where the fermentation has continued for a longer period than with bitter or mild ale. It is sometimes known as Old or Burton and is more popular in the winter months.

Stout is a very dark-coloured, well-hopped beer that may be either dry or sweet, more often the latter.

Most beers are now available in bottle and are often the carbonated and pasteurised versions of their brewer's draught beers. Thus *light ale* is the bottled equivalent of ordinary bitter, then there is *pale ale* or *IPA* (best bitter), *brown ale* (mild), *barley wine* or *strong ale*, and *stout* (rarely on draught except for Guinness). A few bottled beers are not pasteurised and can be improved with keeping, when a yeast sediment develops in the bottom of the bottle. Canned beers are the same as bottled beers, but will never improve in the tin.

When it comes to trying the various beers of Britain in some of the pubs mentioned in the text, you should bear in mind that pubs are usually open in the morning between around 10.30 a.m. and 2.30 p.m. and again in the evening from 5.30 or 6.00 p.m. until 10.30 p.m. The opening hours differ from one locality to another. In central London, for instance, they are normally 11.00 a.m.–3 p.m. and 5.30–11.30 p.m., but in a suburb like Wimbledon the pubs close at 10.30 p.m. On a Saturday closing time may be extended by half an hour. By special arrangement with the licensing Justices an evening or other time extension may be permitted, particularly at holiday time. In country areas or where a pub is near the market, the hours may be varied for those trading at the market; this can include a particularly early start to the day, though we have more often seen food than traditional beer being served at such an hour! Special but regular times outside the usual hours are frequently announced on a wall of the pub.

In Scotland, the licensing laws differ from those in England, and the usual opening hours are from 11.00 p.m. to 2.30 p.m., and from 5.00 p.m. to 10.00 p.m. Few pubs are open later than 10.00 p.m., and none have Sunday licences, although hotel bars are usually open. There also exist some traditional 'brewer's holidays', where you will be lucky to find a bar open at all in certain areas, including hotel bars.

The average pub has both a public bar and a saloon bar. Bitter and mild are the usual draught choices in the former, which is generally furnished simply and where darts, dominoes and cribbage are encouraged. By comparison the saloon bar is decorated more lavishly and the beer is a little more expensive. A lounge bar started as the enclave of residents to the pub and is accordingly more richly decorated. Some pubs have a back room, occasionally called the 'Snug' or even a special 'Ladies Bar' from the days when women ordered port and lemon or drank stout in their own company.

Brewing was—and is—a master craft, and each area, even each town, had its own distinctive beers. For many years local ale-houses brewed their own beer. This developed during the course of the 18th century to a trade whereby one publican would supply a number of neighbouring pubs. It was a local trade because of transport difficulties, but with the introduction of bottling and the improvement in the keeping qualities of beer, brewery companies emerged. Good examples of this were Worthington and Co., who started brewing in 1744, and Bass and Co., founded three years later, in Burton-on-Trent. With improved transport, individual breweries were able to extend their trading areas and the more enterprising bought up public houses and gradually acquired smaller brewery companies.

In the last 25 years the process of take-overs and amalgamations has accelerated, reducing the number of independent breweries from over a thousand to under one hundred. The take-over of breweries usually involves the take-over of pubs, and in 1975, while there are still many free houses, the vast majority of pubs in Britain are controlled by brewers, and of these 'tied houses' by far the greatest number belong to the 'Big Six', the six national brewery companies. These companies have pubs and hotels throughout the country and produce a high proportion of Britain's total beer output. A seventh company, Guinness, is large in production, but owns only one pub. The beers of these national brewers are made for a country-wide market, aimed to please the widest spectrum of beer drinkers, intended to be the same wherever they are served. Hence they have no regional characteristics and, to ensure that they do not alter in transit over long distances, they are usually finely filtered and pasteurised, thus reducing the flavour even more.

The names of these national brewers, with the name signs they use most often are: Allied (Ansells, Aylesbury [ABC], Benskins, Friary Meux, Ind Coope, Tetley); Bass-Charrington (Mitchells & Butlers, Tennent Caledonian, Welsh Brewers, Worthington); Watneys (Dryborough, Samuel Webster, Wilson); Courage (Hole, Simonds, John Smith, Plymouth,

Warwick and Richardson); Scottish and Newcastle (McEwan, Younger); Whitbread (Bentley, Brickwood, Dutton, Flowers, Lacon, Mew Langton, Starkey, Knight and Ford, Strong, Fremlin, Threlfall, Woodlesford).

Truman of London, together with Watney, now belong to Grand Metropolitan Hotels, while the Courage Group belongs to Imperial Tobacco. This is all some way from the small craftsman brewer.

One former head brewer of a Watney subsidiary company recently commented: 'It had got to the stage in the industry where we were brewing by committee. The market research men said what they wanted, then the accountants and everyone else. It seems the brewer's palate came a long way down the line.'

Bill Urquhart, whose words these are, has now established his own small brewery in a village near Northampton, and finds the demand more than he can currently cope with. There still remain independent brewers like Bill Urquhart, who generally supply a well-defined area, and have, on the whole, retained their traditional approach to brewing, and it is to introduce these brews of character, to describe something of their history and to guide you towards the local beers, wherever you may be, that we have written this book. Our philosophy is that there is no point in seeking out in Cornwall the very same beer that you will find in London or Lancaster. Not everyone will like every beer, but at least it is worth trying the local, individual brew.

We have tried to include every brew available, together with some examples of pubs where the beer can be found, though more attention has been given to areas, such as West Country and Wales, which are most likely to be visited by holiday-makers. The Appendix lists all the pubs mentioned by region and county, with the beer available at each.

We would like to thank all those in the brewing business, brewers and publicans, who helped us with information and advice. It would be invidious to name individuals out of so many helpful people. The sources of all the photographs are acknowledged in the captions.

We now hope all our readers will, with the aid of this book, find many places to sample, as George Borrow wrote: 'Good ale, the true and proper drink of Englishmen.'

CG, WK

London

London has long been an important brewing centre, and as
late as 1950 there were over twenty different breweries, now
nearly all swallowed up by the 'Big Six' national brewers. The
signs you are likely to see most are the bright red and white
of Watneys, who have two breweries in London; an old 19th-
century building in Whitechapel in the East End and their
modern headquarters at Mortlake on the south bank of the
Thames. Bass-Charrington whose red triangle, the oldest
registered trade mark in the world (1875), is to be seen
everywhere, still brew at present in the East End at the
Charrington brewery, Mile End. All their pubs serve the
widely advertised Worthington 'E' and Bass as keg beers,
but a few—those which belonged to the Bass-Worthington
company before the merger with Charrington—have the
traditional draught version of this famous beer brewed at
Burton-on-Trent. It is quite a different drink when it does
not come out of the pressurised keg.

In Central London you can find the draught Worthington
or Bass in such pubs as *The Rose* in Hatton Garden, EC1.
This is a fascinating area, where the diamond merchants are
traditionally centred, just beside the real working-class open-
air market of Leather Lane. The Rose is an Edwardian pub,
nothing special in décor, with a clientele of workers and
shoppers from the market and from the small local businesses.
There is a good array of snacks, but the landlord is especially
proud of his beer.

Another pub worth a visit for this beer is *The Black
Friar* on the corner of Queen Victoria Street and New Bridge
Street, EC4, opposite Blackfriars Bridge. It is a curious
wedge-shaped building next to a railway bridge. Though
built in 1903, the pub is said to stand on the site of the chapel
of the priory of the Black Friars, the Dominicans. The
interior is a fascinating example of *art nouveau*, with reliefs
in copper on marble over the bars. *The King's Arms* (Finch's)

at 190 Fulham Road, SW6 (at the west end due north of Battersea Bridge) also has Burton-brewed Bass as well as the London Charrington bitter. It is a plain Victorian pub, with many old mirrors and wooden bar tops; quite a different world from the King's Road pubs not far away.

Charrington's London bitter is to be found in most of their pubs. If you want traditional draught IPA (best) you can find it in the *Royal Connaught* in High-Holborn, WC1, a fairly small, plain pub distinguished by a friendly welcome from the landlord Mike Kennedy and his wife Anne, who have an excellent buffet and restaurant; or in *The Coach and Horses*, Hill Street, W1, close to Berkeley Square. Best avoided on Friday lunch-times, when it is taken over by the advertising fraternity from nearby agencies, it is usually a restful place in the evening. *The Turk's Head* in Motcomb Street, SW1, near Belgrave Square and handy for the Carlton Tower, is another Charrington pub of character. A long narrow bar has at one end an open fireplace with book-lined shelves on either side, like a comfortable drawing room.

You will have no difficulty in finding beers brewed by the other national breweries in most parts of London. Probably the most distinctive are those of Courage, who brew in London near Tower Bridge. Their Director's Bitter is worth looking for, but is not in many pubs. One place where it is to be found is *The Roebuck* in King's Road, SW3, a busy pub with a varied clientele but friendly. Courage also brew the famous 'Imperial Russian Stout', very dark and strong, quite different from the ubiquitous Guinness and well worth a try. Whitbread's beers have been brewed in the City of London since the 18th century. Parts of the existing brewery at Chiswell Street, just on the northern edge of the City boundary, date back to 1750. The Whitbread family was a well-known one in City affairs and is still associated with the company. There are now Whitbread breweries all over the country, but much of the ordinary bitter and mild sold in their London houses is brewed in London. Deliveries in the area round the brewery are still made by horse-drawn drays. Perhaps the most striking of Whitbread's beers is 'Gold Label', a golden barley wine which comes in small 'nip' bottles. It is very strong and not too sweet.

None of the other national brewers brews in London, though Ind Coope, who own many London pubs, do have a brewery at Romford in Essex. Scottish and Newcastle

in Chiswick High Road, and *The Coach and Horses*, on lovely Kew Green not far from Kew Gardens. Young's beer is sometimes found in free houses, so it is worth examining what beer is on sale when you go into such a pub.

The other independent brewer in London is the firm of FULLER, SMITH AND TURNER of Chiswick. You see their Griffin Brewery on the main road to London Airport. It has been in existence since the 17th century, and first came into the Fuller family in 1832. Mr John Fuller was later joined by Mr Henry Smith and Mr John Turner, who had both been brewing in Romford. The brewery stands alongside a huddle of largely 18th-century red-brick buildings between the A4 and the Thames by Chiswick roundabout. Right beside it runs Church Street, a beautiful, secluded street of mellow houses, leading to Chiswick Mall on the river.

Fullers are noted for their draught best bitter, called London Pride. In addition to this and their ordinary bitter and mild, they brew a third draught bitter, E.S.B. (Extra Special Bitter). London Pride—especially if not given too much gas in dispensing—is a full-flavoured, quite hoppy bitter. E.S.B. is also very distinctive in taste and is exceptionally strong—one of the strongest draught bitters in Britain.

Fuller's houses are found mainly on the west side of London, where they are fairly easy to find around Hammersmith, Chiswick and Brentford. In Central London you can try Fuller's beer in *The Star* in Belgrave Mews West, SW1. This is tucked away at the back of Belgrave Square, near Hyde Park Corner, and is one of the few pubs to serve Fuller's draught from handpump. There is also the *Churchill Arms*, in Kensington Church Street, W8, which, apart from the beer, features souvenirs of Sir Winston's war-time career. *The Rossetti* in Queen's Grove, St John's Wood (not far from Lord's, if you have just been to the cricket), is more like an Italian restaurant than a pub, and it does serve meals, but here, too, you can get a pint of London Pride. Fuller's best-known pub must surely be *The Dove* in Upper Mall, Chiswick. This riverside pub has a terrace overlooking the Thames near Hammersmith Bridge. It is an historic building with a number of little rooms off the main bar. It is, unfortunately, almost too popular, but worth a visit. A little farther out, handily situated for Hampton Court Palace, is another historic Fuller's pub, the *Cardinal Wolsey*, on the Green, Hampton Court. It is about 200 yards along Hampton Court Road from the roundabout north of Hampton Court Bridge. Refurbished inside quite comfortably, it has lost some of its former charm. In Richmond, *The Sun Inn* in Parkshot, not far from the Richmond Theatre, is an unspoiled friendly pub, with a wide mixture of customers—well worth a visit. The *Bell and Crown* is a simple but comfortable pub beside the Thames at Strand-on-the-Green near Kew Bridge, but it provides well-kept beer, though on pressure, and good snacks. The yard outside has tables and chairs providing a peaceful seat over-looking the river. If you want to enjoy Fuller's beers in smarter surroundings you can always try the *Master Robert Motel*, on the Great West Road at Heston, not too far from London airport.

In the London area you can sometimes find beers from other regional brewers. They are usually to be found in free houses. For instance, MARSTON'S of Burton-on-Trent, whose pubs are scattered all over the country, has one in Central London. Probably the best-known pub in London and, sadly, in nearly every tourist itinerary, it is nevertheless a fine old house. It is *Ye Olde Cheshire Cheese* in Wine Office Court, Fleet Street, EC4. Its history began in 1538, when it was *The Horn Tavern*. The ground floor contains a restaurant and a cosy bar with an open fire in winter, and sawdust on the uneven board floor, where Marston's best beer, Draught Pedigree, is served. It is a rambling old place, with restaurants also on the first and second floors, and a cellar wine bar.

SHEPHERD NEAME'S Kentish beers are to be found in their one pub in Central London, *The Bishop's Finger* in Smithfield Market. Busy at lunch-time, it is nevertheless good for a snack lunch and a pint of Draught Abbey (Shepherd Neame's keg bitter) or Master Brew bitter, or a more expensive lunch in the restaurant upstairs.

One or two exceptional free houses have a selection of beers from outside London. *The Dive Bar*, 24 Southwark Street, SE1 (hard to find, it is in the basement of a large old building soon to be demolished), has RUDDLE'S beer from Oakham, Rutland, Shepherd Neame's best bitter and THEAKSTON'S Yorkshire beer. This last is a rarity in the south. *The Anglesea Arms* in Selwood Terrace, SW7, off Fulham Road, is a very popular drinkers' pub with a pleasant atmosphere. On a summer evening you can sit on the steps outside. Within they serve Ruddle's best 'County' bitter, Young's and draught Bass. Finally, *The White Horse*, on Parson's Green,

SW6, right at the end of King's Road, opposite the *Duke of Cumberland*, has an unfashionable but comfortable dark wood interior (look at the 19th-century stained-glass window at the back of the pub). Here also you can enjoy Ruddle's beer, and Young's.

The list of guides to London pubs is never ending. There are trendy pubs, and flashy pubs and rough pubs and 'pubby' pubs. The ones mentioned here have been chosen because between them they offer pretty well the complete range of British beer to be obtained in London. They have been selected for their well-kept beer and because of some particular character in the pub.

WK

Southern England

Essex, Herts, Surrey, Kent, Sussex, Hampshire

In those 'home counties' to the north and east of London, Essex and Hertfordshire, you will still see a number of brewers' names not to be found anywhere else, though there are now only three independent breweries operating in the area.

Once away from the flat marshes along the Thames estuary, the Essex countryside is green and rolling, abounding in narrow winding lanes through fields of corn or turnips, where you may suddenly come across a tiny hamlet with its small medieval church, often of flint with a wooden bell-cote, and, of course, its village inn.

It seems appropriate that small country breweries should supply these locals and, often, they do. Signs to look for are those of Ridley, Gray and Rayment.

T. D. RIDLEY AND SONS have their brewery in the village of **Hartford End**, half-way between Chelmsford and Great Dunmow on the B1417. Sited beside a tiny stream, the brewery developed originally from a water mill, and the company has been brewing for 130 years. Ridley's pubs are to be found in and around Chelmsford and as far north as Saffron Walden. They make a feature of their 'beer from the wood', bitter and mild, although they also make keg bitter and mild (called Dagger) and some excellent bottled ales, especially the strong Old Bob.

Gray's of Chelmsford, who produced fine, flavoury beers, suffered from the death-duty blow, which has been the end of many family businesses, and stopped brewing in September 1974. The Gray name will still be seen for a long time yet on pubs in Essex, but the beer inside will be Greene King's from Bury St Edmunds, or Ridley's. For some time Gray's had been producing only draught beer, and the bottled beer in their houses was supplied by Ridley. So now, under the Gray's sign you will find Greene King's draught mild, bitter and keg, and Ridley's bottled ales. Greene King's is a very distinctive beer from Suffolk, so it, too, is a local brew, and a good one.

You will find Ridley's pubs in some of the most unspoiled villages in Essex. **Felsted** is such a one. Only two miles north of the brewery itself, on the road to Great Dunmow, the village is worth a detour for its fine 16th- and 17th-century buildings, in particular, the Old School House, which faces the High Street. Behind the school is the flint church, and opposite, on one corner, is a fascinating half-timbered house with a deep overhang and carving along the horizontal first-floor beam. On the corner is a painted figure of a woman with cloven hoofs and along one beam are the words 'George Boote made this house 1596'. It is now a restaurant. On the opposite corner stands the not unpleasing neo-Tudor *Swan Hotel*. Comfortably furnished, it serves the excellent Ridley's bitter and mild out of wooden barrels. It also has rooms and an attractive restaurant. On the southern edge of the village is the *Yew Tree*, a small and simple Victorian red-brick pub, with a pretty garden with apple trees.

One of the first places in which I tried Ridley's beer was in *The Thatcher's Arms*, a welcoming little pub, set back off the road by itself outside the minute hamlet of **Radley Green**. To get there you look for the signs on the A122 road about half-way between Chipping Ongar and Chelmsford. Publican Steve Thomas, who told me he had once run a Watney's pub, said he liked being a tenant of a small brewery. He felt things were more efficient as well as pleasanter. 'In the old place I used to get three separate deliveries; first keg beer; then tank beer; then the bottled beer, each lorry with three men. Ridley's deliver everything in one go with two men. And when one's on holiday his mate delivers alone.' *The Thatcher's Arms* is small and attractively decorated and does excellent hot and cold snacks. The beer is drawn direct from the barrels behind the bar. There is a garden with a swing. Sadly there are no rooms, as it would make a most peaceful place to stay.

In **Chelmsford** Ridley's beer can be found in some half a dozen pubs, including *The Ship* in Broomfield Road. It is not hard to find in this small county town. On the road northwards, towards Great Dunmow (A130), some five miles out of Chelmsford lies the straggling village of **Great Waltham**. Its most striking building as you enter from the south is a lovely red-brick Elizabethan house, with the characteristic tall 16th-century chimneys. Next to this is the large flint-built church and round the bend on the left is *The Beehive*. It is one of Ridley's post-war pubs, a low rather rambling, plain building, very much the village local. Opposite is the pretty *Six Bells*, but it serves Ind Coope's beer. A more attractive building is the *Green Man*, a Ridley's house at **Howe Street**, just a mile north of Great Waltham. On the right of the main road, it is a large, white-painted pub, obviously well cared for, whose pretty dining-room has dark polished wooden tables. Other Ridley's pubs include *The Black Lion* at **High Roding**. When last seen it had no sign, but the brewer's name was clear enough and the house itself is a fine half-timbered building on the main B184 from Chipping Ongar to Great Dunmow. The Italian proprietor, Mr Ricci, offers good food in the restaurant as well as a friendly welcome. At **Great Dunmow**, on the north edge of the village, you can drink Ridley's in *The Cricketers* on Beaumont Hill, which also has a steak bar and, farther north again, in the beautiful picturebook village of **Finchingfield**, the *Red Lion*, an old inn on Church Hill, offers food and rooms, as well as Ridley's beer.

Gray's signs, which now mean Greene King's draught beers, are to be seen quite easily in **Chelmsford**, where the brewery still stands near the town centre. Elsewhere they are often found in small towns, such as **Maldon**, where the *Queen's Head*, set attractively near the River Blackwater, has good snacks. In the same town are *The Carpenter's Arms* and the *Swan Hotel*, which has a restaurant and rooms. Also in Maldon, Adnams' fine beers from Southwold in Suffolk can be found at the *Blue Boar*. This is one of the few outlets for Adnams' in Essex, but their free trade is increasing, so it is worthwhile enquiring in a free house to see if they have Adnams' beers.

One of the pleasantest of Gray's houses is *The Shepherd* at **Kelvedon Hatch**, three miles north of Brentwood on the A128. It claims to be 500 years old and was apparently frequented by the 18th-century highwayman Jack Shepherd. In the little town of **Chipping Ongar** on the A113, a pleasant, if slow, road out of London through Woodford and Chigwell, *The Cock Tavern* is worth a visit. A weatherboarded pub in the high street, it is an old building which has been redecorated and enlarged, but without spoiling its warm and cosy character.

RAYMENT'S of Furneux Pelham, near **Buntingford**, Herts, is another small country brewery. Owned for over forty years by

Greene King, they nevertheless have continued brewing their own beers, which have a quite different appeal from those of Greene King.

Just west of the village of Furneux Pelham stands Furneux Pelham Hall, an Elizabethan manor house, where there was many years ago a small brewing concern. Some 130 years ago, however, William Rayment, a local farmer, took on the lease of the Hall. He developed the brewing into a lively concern, until 1860, when the lease ended and he had to move to another site in the village. Here he built a new brewery, largely, it seems, of local bricks. There is no longer a Rayment concerned with the business, for the Lake family took over control early in this century. Being farmers as well, the Lakes were able to provide the brewery with their own local-grown barley. Greene, King and Sons bought the business in 1928, but the family continued to run it, and Captain H. N. Lake remained a director until very recently.

You can try Rayment's beer in a number of villages round Furneux Pelham. In the north-west of Essex near the A11 they have three houses at **Stansted**, *The Dog and Duck* in Lower Street, *The Ash* at Burton End and *The Cock* in Silver Street. They are all quite simple, but handy if you are making for Stansted airport. Farther north is the lovely old town of **Thaxted**. It should not be missed for its wealth of old buildings, in particular, the medieval half-timbered buildings of Church Street, leading uphill to the large flint-built church, with its fine porch and tower. Opposite the church is *The Swan Hotel*, mainly a late-18th-century building, where you will find a friendly welcome. It is a free house, so, as well as Rayment's bitter on draught, there are also seven keg beers, almost all the nationally known names. It is a residential house and has a restaurant, as well as serving bar snacks. At the southern end of the town, as you come in along the A130, there is a sign to 'The Bardfields' along a minor road. About a mile along here is the tiny hamlet of **Bardfield End Green**. Across the Green, with its cricket field in summer, is a small village pub, *The Butcher's Arms*. In process of having a face lift when I visited it, it looks likely still to keep its friendly simplicity, and the Rayment's beer will undoubtedly still be well kept.

Saffron Walden is another Essex town with great character, and here Rayment's pubs include *The Axe and Compass* in Ashden Road and *The Gate* in Thaxted Road.

At **Newport** on the A11 near Saffron Walden Rayments have *The White Horse*. Just to the west of Newport at the oddly named **Wicken Bonhunt**, the *Coach and Horses* is a pleasing pub.

In Hertfordshire, try Rayment's at *The White Lion*, **Sawbridgeworth** (on the A11 north of Harlow). At this residential hotel on the corner of Bell Street, Mr Mansell serves snacks as well as full meals. *The White Horse* at **Hatfield Heath** just east of Sawbridgeworth is a simple little pub overlooking the cricket green. At **Furneux Pelham** itself the *Brewery Tap* is, as you would expect, very close to the brewery, but *The Star* is perhaps a more typical Rayment's pub.

Farther north, on the B1368 road to Cambridge, *The Tally Ho* is a plain but pleasant house on the right just outside **Barkway**. In all, Rayments have only some thirty pubs, but you may also find their beer in free houses.

The biggest of the independent brewers in Essex and Hertfordshire are McMULLEN AND SONS. In **Hertford**, the pleasant county town, McMullen's have been brewing since 1827, when Peter McMullen set up his first small brewery in Back Street, now Railway Street. Ever since there has been a McMullen at the helm and business has steadily expanded. The present brewery in Hartham Lane in the centre of town was built in 1891, and one of the features of advertisements publicising this event was that the brewery possessed 'water of the utmost purity from an artesian well of great depth'. Good clear water is an important factor in beer-making, and many breweries have their own wells. Water has its own special qualities, depending on the ground from which it comes, and contributes to the individual flavours of beers from different regions.

McMullen's now have about 200 houses within a radius of thirty miles from Hertford. This is a delivery area that suits the traditional brewer, enabling him to provide a regular service and ensure that the beer is kept in good condition. McMullen's are the only completely independent brewery remaining in Hertfordshire, and their beers can also be found in pubs in the surrounding counties of Essex, Middlesex and Bedfordshire.

Like most family brewers, McMullen's are able to keep in close touch with their tenants and, through a regular newsletter, also offer advice and hints to their publicans on how to improve their food and service, the appearance of their pub and, most important, how to ensure the beer is well kept. Great stress is laid on the correct serving temperature, neither chilled nor warm. McMullen's find—as do most local brewers—that by far their best selling beer is their draught bitter, called Country Best Bitter. It is increasing its sales by comparison with keg bitter and draught mild, which used to be more popular. McMullen's AK draught mild is not too sweet, and their Castle Keg is chilled and filtered but not pasteurised, which may be why, to my taste, it has more flavour than most keg beer. In bottle they have the equivalent ales, but are especially proud of Mitre, a strong pale ale, and Olde Time, an extra strong ale.

In **Hertford** itself you can try McMullen's in *The Salisbury Arms*, an attractive 15th-century residential hotel in Fore Street.

On the A10 at **Wormley**, south of Broxbourne, a useful place for a snack is McMullen's *The Old Star*. It has been tarted up a little as a 'theme' pub, but is comfortable and welcoming. At **Ware**, *The French Horn* in the High Street is an old house, which retains some original features, notably a Jacobean staircase. The landlord does a good selection of soups and salads. North of Ware, still on the Cambridge Road, is *The Lamb and Flag* at **Colliers End**. An unpretentious pub by the roadside, it serves good hot and cold snacks. The AK mild is served by handpump, but the draught bitter is under top pressure.

In **Puckeridge**, a lovely old village now happily by-passed by the A10, the *White Hart* stands at the fork where the main Cambridge road and the winding B1368 part company. It is an old building with the kind of cosy brass-gleaming interior one likes to think typical of a country inn; well worth a stop for a pint of McMullen's before taking the more leisurely way to Cambridge.

Much Hadham is another quiet village in the pretty countryside between the A10 and A11. At **Perry Green**, a mile or so to the south, McMullen's have a quiet country inn, *The Hoops*, where full meals and snacks at the bar are available at almost any time. A much simpler village pub is *The Green Man* at **Widford**, some two miles south.

Around the A1 trunk road in the west of the county, McMullen's signs can be seen in **Hatfield**, **Stevenage**, **Welwyn** and **St Albans**. In this last place, a very simple little local is the *Farrier's Arms* in Lower Dagnall Street, while a smarter pub is *The Blue Anchor*, Fishpool Street, near the town centre.

McMullen's beers extend into north London and Essex; they can be found at *The Royal Oak*, Kings Head Hill, **Chingford**, on the southern edge of Epping Forest, and at *The Cricketers*, High Road, **Woodford Green**, just near the A11.

Apart from their supply of draught beer to Gray's pubs, Greene King have a number of their own houses in Essex and Herts, mainly in the north and east. Their strong draught Abbott Ale takes some beating, when you can find it. One particularly charming pub is *The Swan* at **Little Henny**, a minute village on the Essex bank of the Stour between Bures and Sudbury. The tiny bar parlour is cosy and friendly and there are indeed swans on the river. By the coast, you can enjoy Greene King at **Holland on Sea**, next to **Clacton** (at the *Kingscliff*), and in Clacton itself in *The Black Bull*, St Osyph Road; while in the little resort of **Brightlingsea**, there is *The Cherry Tree*, a pleasant pub with rooms to let. Greene King pubs can be found also in **Braintree** (*The Bull* in Market Place and *Waggon and Horses* in South Street) and at **Coggeshall**, an attractive old former coaching village on the main road from Braintree to Colchester, the old Roman Stane Street. Here the sign is *The King's Arms* on Broad Green, about a mile and a half to the west of the village.

Colchester does not offer a wide choice of local brews, but Adnam's now have *The British Grenadier*, a name which suits this army-influenced town. Tolly-Cobbold's beer from Ipswich can be found here at *The Buck's Horn*. Tolly Cobbold also have a house, *The White Horse*, in **Great Dunmow**, a plain little town pub in the high street.

Of the counties adjoining London on the south, Surrey alone no longer has any genuinely local beer. It is now at least twenty years since Friary Ales were brewed in Guildford, and the company which succeeded Friary, Meux of London, has also been swallowed up by Allied Breweries, which explains why there are so many Ind Coope pubs in the county. You will still see a few of the old Friary/Meux signs, but the beer is now Ind Coope's, from Burton, or sometimes from Romford, Essex.

Individual beers from London and neighbouring counties can be found in Surrey, however, though somewhat thinly scattered. Near London, national brewers' signs predominate, especially Courage, though in the west of the county some of their pubs do have draught beer brewed at Reading, which has a little more character. YOUNG's of Wandsworth have acquired several houses in Surrey, and increasingly their excellent beers are found in free houses.

Coming into Surrey through the London suburbs, one place you might wish to race through is **Surbiton**, although there are vestiges of Surbiton's former existence as a coaching stage. From the A3, turn west at Tolworth Tower at the sign for Surbiton, and some two miles along this road at the bottom of Surbiton Hill you will see a Young's sign on the right. It is *The Waggon & Horses*, built some 200 years ago to provide horses for the climb up the hill. It was originally built at the old Toll Gate, long since gone: the pub itself was rebuilt in 1888 to provide rooms for the grand visitors to the new Assembly Rooms opposite. This life has now passed Surbiton by and the *Waggon & Horses* no longer has rooms, but it makes you welcome in its large but cosy bars.

Farther south on the A3, a turning to the east leads to **Claygate**, where Young's have *The Foley Arms*, a comfortably-furnished pub, while in the centre of **Esher**, well placed for Sandown Races, is a fine old inn, *The Bear*. At **Epsom**, in East Street, Young's *King's Arms* is a simpler, 'pubby' kind of pub. Farther out into the country along the Guildford–Dorking road at **Gomshall** is *The Black Horse*, a friendly house, ideal for a snack or full meal; the Special Bitter is well kept. At the next village of **Shere**, Young's have *The Prince of Wales*, a fairly simple house in a picturesque village, with pleasant walks in the Red Downs. The pub is in the middle of the village, which is now off the main A25. Young's beer can also be drunk in a smarter free house, *The Onslow Arms*, at **West Clandon**, some three miles north-east of Guildford.

Guildford has no local beer, but one or two houses serve Courage's Reading beer, including *The Two Brewers* in Castle Street, while at **Shalford**, just to the south, *The Sea Horse* has Gale's beer from Hampshire, and also serves bar lunches. This is certainly worth a detour for the beer alone. North of Guildford on the A3 at **Ripley**, one little Courage pub should be visited. It is *The Ship* in the High Street, a 'front-parlour' pub with simple décor but a warm welcome and good sandwiches.

To find any but national beers elsewhere in Surrey, you have to go to the southern border with Sussex.

Just inside Surrey you can find the Horsham Ales sign of King and Barnes near **Cranleigh** at *The Leathern Bottle* on the Guildford–Horsham road, A281, and at **Leigh** (pronounced locally 'Lie') at *The Plough*, a pleasant country pub with good snacks about three miles south-west of Reigate. In the town of **Horley** just north of Gatwick Airport, Horsham Ales can be found at *The Gatwick* in the High Street.

GALE's beer from Horndean, near Portsmouth, can also be found in some pubs in the south-west of Surrey. As well as at Shalford, mentioned above, they have *The Red Lion* at **Milford** on the A3 near Godalming, a pleasant inn on London Road, which serves bar lunches and snacks. Farther south down the A3, *The Three Horse Shoes* at **Thursley** and *The Fox and Pelican* at **Grayshott** near Hindhead offer the distinctive Gale's ales and a pleasant snack. *The Fox and Pelican* offers full meals in its restaurant. You can also try Gale's at *The Woodcock Inn*, Beacon Hill, near **Hindhead**, and, further west, there is an oasis for the seeker after real beer at *The Queen's Head*, The Borough, **Farnham**.

The county of West Sussex is the home of KING AND BARNES' Horsham Ales. The brewery is situated in the old market town of Horsham, now very much in the commuter belt, but still full of character. Horsham draught bitter is very individual in flavour and is brewed in the traditional way, with the final addition of dry hops. Also brewed are a dark mild and an Old Ale, which is a strong dark beer usually brewed only in winter. Among the bottled beers is a sweet stout—JK stout —named after the founder, James King.

King and Barnes have nearly sixty houses, all round Horsham and into Surrey. In **Horsham** itself, pubs worth a visit are *The Bear*, a comfortable pub in Market Square, and the strangely-named *Dog and Bacon* on North Parade. About five miles south-east at **Lower Beeding** on the A279 is *Crabtree Inn* and farther on, beyond the Brighton Road, in the picturesque village of **Ardingly**, is *The Avins Bridge Hotel*.

On the Horsham–Guildford road the *Fox Inn* at **Bucks Green**, a small village on the River Arun, is a King and Barnes house. In the country to the west, *The Onslow Arms* at **Loxwood** on the B2133 is a country inn with a welcoming atmosphere.

Petworth is an historic town, noted especially for the National Trust property of Petworth House, a striking 17th-century house in a large deer park, with a fine collection of pictures and furniture. After your visit to the house a pint of K and B bitter at *The Horseguards* in **Tillington** will go down well; it is just a mile to the west. Small and comfortable, the pub faces the church about a hundred yards off the main road. Farther along this road lies another lovely country town, Midhurst. Just before you reach the town is the famous polo centre, Cowdray Park, with a magnificent house and grounds. In the village of **Easebourne** next to the park you will find *The Rother Inn*, a pleasant King and Barnes pub.

In **Midhurst** a different brewer's sign can be seen on *The Angel*, an AA two-star hotel in North Street. This is Gale's Horndean Ales, from Hampshire. They have several pubs around Midhurst, including *The Shamrock Inn* at **Bepton**, a tiny village off the A186 to the south, and *The Greyhound* at **Cocking Causeway** on the A286.

Gale's beer is easily found in **Chichester** too. For those who want a drink and a meal after looking at the Cathedral or before a visit to the Chichester Theatre, there is *The Cattle Market Inn*, which serves meals, in the Hornet on the corner of Market Avenue or *The Eastgate Inn*, also in the Hornet, which has snacks to go with its beer.

King and Barnes country also extends east of Chichester. A charming village in which to enjoy their beer is **West Chiltington**, off the beaten track, about four miles east of Pulborough. The *Elephant and Castle* there has a beer garden, for when the weather is kind.

For a pleasant diversion off the road to Worthing you could do worse than take the right fork on to the B2224 south of Horsham, then turn right again one and a half miles farther on into the hamlet of **Dragon's Green**. The local is, naturally, called *George and Dragon*. It is a simple pub, where the King and Barnes beer is well kept. In **Worthing**, not noted for a good selection of beer, King and Barnes ales can be found in *The Jolly Brewers*.

Finally, we should mention the nearest King and Barnes pub to Brighton, *The Bridge Inn* at **Upper Beeding** on the A283 not far from Steyning.

If Horsham Ales are the beers of West Sussex, HARVEY's of Lewes are the brewers for East Sussex. **Lewes** is the county town of this portion of the county, set on the downs north of the coastal resorts of Brighton and Eastbourne. Lewes has always been a brewing town; until the end of the First World War, there were no fewer than seven breweries in this little town. Now only two companies remain, Harvey and BEARD. However, though each have their own pubs, and, in fact, there are more Beard's signs about than Harvey's, Beard no longer make their own beer. All the beer is brewed by Harvey's, even though some bottles have Beard's labels.

Harvey's are a typical small family brewery. Founded in 1790 by John Harvey (no relation to the sherry firm of that name), the company is still controlled by his descendants. They still brew in the traditional way using just malt, sugar and hops, and in many pubs the beer is dispensed by hand-pumps or straight out of the barrel. In a number of places carbon dioxide is put on top of the beer, to prevent air getting into it, but it is not usually a strong pressure and does not get into the beer to make it gassy. The brewery is easily seen in Lewes, the brewing tower standing out among a huddle of buildings by the river. The original fermenting block and cellars of 1790 are still in use, but the brewhouse and tower were built in 1880 to the designs of William Bradford, whose work can be seen in several breweries built at this period.

Harvey's brew an ordinary and a best bitter, a particularly full-flavoured, bitter beer, as well as a mild. They do a keg beer, which is the best bitter, chilled and filtered, and occasionally on draught is Elizabethan Ale, a very strong barley wine. The best bitter is, predictably, their best-selling beer.

In Lewes, of course, there is no difficulty in finding a Beard's or Harvey's house. Two worth trying are *The Black Horse Hotel* and *The Lamb Hotel*, both under Beard's signs.

On the coast at **Eastbourne**, not an easy place to find a distinctive pint, there are several Harvey's pubs, mainly away from the sea-front and usually fairly plain, but the beer and the welcome are excellent. One such pub is the *Hurst Arms* in Willingdon Road, on the main road out to the north. *The Terminus Hotel*, Terminus Road, has been done up, is comfortable and serves good lunch-time snacks. For a really pretty, quiet setting for a drink, you can do no better than find *The Cricketer's Arms* at **Berwick**, a small local with a pretty garden in a tiny hamlet, just off the main A27, three miles west of Polegate. It is only a short way from here to the prehistoric Long Man of Wilmington, a figure cut in the chalk on the north side of the downs.

A roadside house that does snacks is *The Golden Cross* at **Chiddingly** on the A22 two miles north-west of Horsebridge, and a little farther north, at **East Hoathly**, Harvey's *Forester's Arms* is a plain red-brick pub, set back from the main road. In **Brighton** you won't find any Harvey's houses, but quite close is *The Black Lion* at **Patcham**, just as you enter the outskirts of Brighton on the A23, and the *Black Horse* is at **Rottingdean** just along the coast. In Brighton itself, however, you can drink Gale's fine Hampshire ales at *Harrison's Bar* in King's Road.

Inland there are several Harvey pubs in and around **Hailsham**, including *The Red Lion* at Magham Down along the road towards Hurstmonceux. Two especially pleasant places at which to drink Harvey's are *The Blackboys* at **Blackboys** east of Uckfield and, farther east, north of Ashdown Forest at *The Dorset Arms* in the little village of **Withyham**, a few miles off the A264.

The most historic of Sussex seaside resorts is **Hastings**, with the remains of its castle on the cliff, its old churches and narrow lanes of medieval houses.

Here you will come across a beer brewed in Kent, that of Shepherd Neame of Faversham. In the old part of Hastings is *The Duke of Wellington* in High Street, while in Cornwallis Street, near the county cricket ground, *The Prince Albert* offers a warm welcome.

The actual site of the battle of 1066 is, of course, a few miles north, where the town of **Battle** grew up around the Abbey founded by William the Conqueror beside the battlefield. Opposite the Abbey Gatehouse, *The Abbey Hotel* offers Shepherd Neame's ales as well as rooms, meals and snacks.

This brings us to the borders of Kent, but to find the present home of Kentish beers, we need to go north.

For a county famous for its hop gardens and oast houses it is sad that the breweries of Kent have long been reduced to only two. Both are in the noted brewing town of **Faversham** in north Kent on the A2, some ten miles on the London side of Canterbury. FREMLIN'S name is still to be found on a number of pubs in Kent, but gradually the 'national' Whitbread's signs are taking over, since Whitbread bought the Fremlin brewery some years ago. Draught bitter is still brewed there, but it is no longer much different from Whitbread's to be found anywhere. The remaining independent brewery is that of SHEPHERD NEAME LTD, whose slogan 'Master Brewers' is commonly seen all around north and east Kent. They brew a good clean-flavoured draught bitter and a slightly stronger best bitter, as well as Draught Abbey, which is, in fact, keg bitter, but has a good flavour. The best bitter in bottle is called Abbey Ale, and they brew a good pale strong ale, Bishop's Finger.

The brewery was founded as early as 1698, four years before the Bank of England, on part of the site of the present brewery. The Shepherd family came into the firm in 1741, and it was Julius Shepherd, son of the first Shepherd to buy the company, who introduced a steam engine into the brewhouse in 1790, the first such engine in the town.

In the mid-19th century Percy Beale Neame came into the firm, and today it is still under the personal control of the Neame family. Their pubs can be found all over the county and in the south-eastern outskirts of London.

In **Faversham** itself, a town with a long history connected with the sea, one of the most interesting of Shepherd Neame's pubs is *The Three Tuns*, in Tanner Street. It is a listed building; here, it is said, Lord Nelson paid off the last of his crew before sailing down Faversham Creek. *The Castle* in West Street, with its bow windows, dates from 1450, while *The Sun* in the same street is another 15th-century building and has a fine old fireplace.

The northern coast of Kent along the Thames Estuary is known mainly for the popular seaside towns of Margate, Herne Bay and Whitstable, but they contain some very attractive old streets and buildings.

On Borstal Hill in **Whitstable**, a 400-year-old pub still stands. Built originally as a forge, *The Four Horseshoes* now dispenses Shepherd Neame ales. In neighbouring **Herne Bay** *The Diver's Arms* on the sea front is said to have been a smugglers' haunt.

Inland a very short distance, you can discover some quiet and charming village inns, such as *The Three Horseshoes* at **Hernhill** about two miles north of the A2 road, three miles east of Faversham. The Shepherd Neame beer is well kept in this 18th-century pub, where you may well see paintings by local artists.

South of here *The White Lion* at **Selling** is a most comfortable and beautifully kept pub in a village in a network of country lanes about 4 miles from the end of the M2 at junction 7. It won the *Evening Standard*'s 'Pub of the Year' award for Shepherd Neame in 1969.

South again on the A252 road to Canterbury lies **Chilham**, a village of old timbered houses on the River Stour. Near the Square is *The Woolpack*, a former coaching inn which serves meals and snacks.

Canterbury is the meeting point of all the roads in the east of Kent. Apart from the magnificent cathedral, there are many beautiful old buildings in the city and, in summer, the St Lawrence County Cricket Ground is perhaps the loveliest in England. There is a Shepherd Neame pub to be found in St Dunstan's Street, among whose half-timbered 17th-century houses stands *The Bishop's Finger*, while the nearest pub to the cathedral is *The Shakespeare*, an old bow-fronted house in Butchery Lane, which also lets rooms.

The north-easterly road out of Canterbury leads to the Isle of Thanet. Conveniently placed for a stop on the road to the Hoverport at Ramsgate's Pegwell Bay is the old *Crown Inn* at **Sarre**, at the junction of the A28 and A253 roads. The building dates from 1500 and is said to be the place where Dickens wrote *Pickwick Papers*. One of its claims to fame is its home-made cherry brandy, made to a Huguenot recipe handed down for 300 years. Be sure to notice the wrought-iron fireplace made in 1650, bearing the Rose of England and Royal Crown.

In the lanes of east Kent between Canterbury and the coast are many lovely villages, usually with old inns. One worth looking for is **Chillenden**, about five miles south-west of Sandwich. A well-preserved windmill stands out in the village, and *The Griffin's Head* is a Tudor pub which serves Shepherd Neame's beers and hot and cold snacks.

Dover has a good selection of pubs, though you need to avoid the main routes to the docks. An interesting one is a residential Shepherd Neame house, *The Lord Nelson* in Flying Horse Lane.

Hythe, on the edge of Romney Marsh, and one terminus of the Romney, Hythe and Dymchurch Light Railway, is one of Kent's oldest towns and a Cinque Port. *The Globe Inn*, High Street, is the place to look for Kentish beer. Near by, along the B2067 road, is **Aldington** village, where *The Walnut Tree* stands on a hill looking across the Marsh. Originally built in the Middle Ages, the inn has associations with local smugglers and is supposed to be on the site of a Roman villa. It has a comfortable restaurant and gardens.

At **Bethersden**, some six miles west of Ashford along the A28, *The Bull*, by the cricket green, offers a good welcome and meals if you want to eat. **Biddenden**, farther west, a village with many 16th-century houses, has *The Chequers*, where you might stop for a drink of Shepherd Neame's Master Brew after a visit to nearby Sissinghurst Castle.

The road north from here takes one to **Sutton Vallence**, where *The Clothworker's Arms* is a reminder that the public school there was a foundation of the Worshipful Company of Clothmakers.

To the north of here runs the A20 main London–Maidstone–Ashford road. It is not always easy to find a restful stopping place along such a busy road, but one can be found at **Lenham**, about half-way between Charing and Maidstone. The village, by-passed by the main road, has a fine square with one particularly beautiful half-timbered building on one corner. It is now a chemist's shop, but inside there is a King post and the original roof beams are visible, as no ceiling has been put in. *The Dog and Bear Inn*, which dates from 1602, presents an 18th-century frontage with a beautiful Queen Anne Coat of Arms above the entrance. There is a cheerful public bar and a cosy, welcoming saloon. The Shepherd Neame bitter and mild is well kept and served by handpump.

In **Maidstone** *The Fisherman's Arms* is worth a visit. The oldest pub in town, it dates from 1430. West of here Shepherd Neame's beer can be found in **Wrotham**, at *The Rose and Crown*, High Street; *The Rose and Crown* is an unpretentious, cosy pub with beer on handpump and good bar snacks. In **Tonbridge** itself is Shepherd Neame's *The Forester's Arms* in George Street. **Tunbridge Wells** does not offer much in the way of local beer, but *The High Brooms Hotel* in the north of the town has Harvey's Sussex beer (under the Beard's sign); there is a Harvey's pub also at **Bell's Yew Green**, near Frant Station south of the town, *The Brecknock Arms*.

Along the Sevenoaks–Westerham road in **Brasted** there is an unexceptional-looking pub in the main street, which should not be passed by. It is *The King's Arms*, which inside is a most cosy, unspoiled pub, with a large inglenook fireplace. The atmosphere is local and friendly and the Shepherd Neame's beers are served by handpump.

Gale's is now the only independent brewery in Hampshire, but at one time anyone travelling south-west from London by train or road was greeted by enormous signs proclaiming 'You are now entering the Strong country'. But Strong, the brewers of Romsey, fell to a Whitbread take-over, and now when you see Strong signs the beer will be Whitbread, though some of the draught beer will come from Romsey. Whitbread also acquired Brickwoods of Portsmouth, so there is no shortage of Whitbread pubs in Hampshire, and especially in Portsmouth or Romsey. Courage is also strongly represented in the county, because at one time they brewed at Alton. Some pubs have Courage's draught beers from Reading.

North of Portsmouth the straggling, not very attractive village of **Horndean** is the place where some of the best of all southern beers are made, by GEORGE GALE AND CO. Gale's are a small independent company, who, because of their size, are able to take a close personal interest in every one of their tenanted houses. Mr E. T. Argyle is both a director of the firm and head brewer. He decides each week what quantity of which beers to produce, and on his experience rests much of the success or failure of the business. Next door to the brewery is *The Ship and Bell*, and here, some 300 years ago, when this main road from London to Portsmouth was often dangerous because of highwaymen and cut-throats, travellers were able to hire servants to protect them on the next stage of their journey. Like many inns, it brewed its own beer, and by about 1720 it had been bought by the Gale family. A new brewery was built opposite the inn, but was later burnt down, leaving only the old Blacksmith's Shop and Carpenter's Shop, now used only for storage. The present Victorian brewery was built in 1869, and despite modernisation retains much of its old appearance.

Gale's brew two bitters (HSB—Horndean Special Bitter, and BBB—ordinary) and two milds, a light and a dark. They also do a small amount of Keg Bitter, mainly for clubs, and a Keg Mild (777). The most unusual of their beers is Prize Old Ale, a strong barley wine, which has a nutty taste, not at all sweet, and is almost still. Only a limited amount is made, as it demands long maturing; it is kept for a year in hogshead and six months after bottling in nips and, almost unique for beer, cork-stoppered half-pint bottles.

Gale's pubs are not hard to find in the area around **Portsmouth** and **Southsea**, where *The India Arms*, in Great Southsea Street, is worth a visit. Of course *The Ship and Bell* next to the brewery at **Horndean** has the beer in excellent condition, while at the village of **Chalton** just two miles off the A3 to the north is a pretty half-timbered country pub, *The Red Lion*. It is worth a detour for a peaceful snack and a pint.

To the west of the A3 on the road to Southampton via Botley, *The King's Head* at **Wickham** offers a warm welcome and a wide selection of food in the bar. Just outside **Botley**, on the A3051, is a simpler pub, *The Horse and Jockey* at **Curbridge**. You can try Gale's beers too in a lovely pub at **Havant**, *The Old House at Home*. Other Gale's houses worth a call include *The Square Brewery*, in the attractive market square at **Petersfield**, and, if you like to get off the main roads for a lunch-time drink, try *The Peat Spade* at **Longstock**, if you are in the vicinity of the A30. It is north of **Stockbridge**, about two miles up the Andover road. Cold snacks are available. Another pleasant Gale's pub, just off the M3, is *The Four Horse Shoes* at **Long Sutton** (one mile to the east of the A32, four miles south of Odiham). The well-kept beer and bar meals make it worth a detour.

In the south and west of the county you begin to find various West Country beers from Dorset and Wiltshire. WADWORTH's of Devizes, who are noted for dispensing their draught beer only by handpump or gravity, have two pubs in Hampshire, both in **Andover**; *The Swallow* in Pilgrim's Way and *Lamb*, Winchester Street. In the same town you will find the sign of MARSTON of Burton upon Trent outside *The Angel Inn*. Marston's houses are scattered throughout the county and are worth seeking for the well-flavoured draught bitter, even when it is served by pressure.

There are several Marston pubs in **Winchester**, notably *The Crown and Anchor*, opposite King Alfred's statue. In the pretty village of **Itchen Abbas**, east of the cathedral city, *The Plough Inn* is well placed for fishing.

In **Southampton**, too, you can try their beer in *The Marsh Hotel*, very close to the Continental Ferry Terminus. In the countryside *The Black Dog* at **Waltham Chase**, south of Bishop's Waltham, is worth a stop for a snack or meal with your drink.

Another name to look for is ELDRIDGE, POPE & Co. of Dorchester, whose Huntsman Ales can be drunk around

Southampton and the New Forest. Look for it at *The Crown Hotel*, **Ringwood**, which has a garden and a children's room. Elsewhere in the New Forest area there is *The Rose and Crown* in **Brockenhurst** and, farther south, in the coastal resort of **Lymington** look for the Eldridge Pope sign at *The Angel Hotel*. Try their beer too at *The Red Lion*, **Boldre**, just to the north.

In **Portsmouth** there are several Eldridge Pope pubs, in particular *The Dorchester Arms* in Market Way.

HALL AND WOODHOUSE of Blandford Forum, Dorset, whose trade-mark is 'Badger Beers', have a few houses in the south and west of the county. North of Ringwood on the Salisbury road near the attractive town of Fordingbridge, *The Churchill Arms* is a pleasant pub in the village of **Alderholt**.

The Isle of Wight has one independent brewery, that of BURT AND CO. of Ventnor. Their Ventnor Ales are found all over the island in many hotels, clubs, holiday camps and free houses, though there are only a few tied houses. Their beers include draught bitter (LB), Special Bitter (VPA), which is more often found, and a mild (BMA). Try Burt's at *The Volunteer* in **Ventnor** and at *The Mill Bay*; it can also be found in **Shanklin** and **Freshwater**.

The national brewers have a strong hold in the island, but there are a few Gale's houses, which, if you have discovered their beer on the mainland, are well worth searching for. In **Ryde** *The Castle* in the High Street and *Simeon Arms* are both Gale's pubs, while they also have *The Commercial Hotel* in St John's Road, **Sandown**.

WK

South-west Midlands
Berkshire, Oxfordshire, Gloucestershire, Wiltshire

The area we are calling here the South-west Midlands includes the lovely countryside of yellow limestone hills, winding streams and old stone towns known as the Cotswolds, which stretches roughly south-west to north-east across much of Oxfordshire and Gloucestershire. To the south, in Berkshire and Wiltshire, lies a different kind of hill country, the rolling chalk downs, with their plentiful evidence of prehistoric man —burial mounds, stone circles such as Stonehenge and figures cut out of the chalk, like the famous White Horse of Uffington.

There is, too, a good variety of beers to be found in the pretty and inviting country pubs and old town inns.

For people coming from London, perhaps the best place to start is in Berkshire, as so much traffic nowadays travels west along the M4. Now that Abingdon has been moved—administratively—from Berkshire to Oxford, there is no independent brewery left in the county. Courage, however, still brew at their Reading brewery, and some of their houses offer the draught mild and bitter through traditional hand-pumps instead of under top pressure. The usual range of bottled and keg beers is available in all their pubs, which are scattered throughout the county.

Of individual local brews to be found in Berkshire, the one you will find most easily is Morland's of Abingdon. MORLAND & Co. started business as long ago as 1711, with two breweries, one in West Ilsley and the other in Abingdon. In the mid-19th century another brewery was added in Abingdon, where the company is now centred. As with most local brewers, Morland gradually absorbed a number of very small companies round about, and now they have over 200 tied houses, mainly in Berkshire, to the south and west of Abingdon and in Oxfordshire. Morland's beers are still brewed in the traditional way, without pasteurising, and draught beer is sent out under finings to the pubs, though it is normally kept under top pressure.

Morlands brew a good sound draught bitter and a slightly stronger and sweeter Best Bitter, as well as a mild. In bottle, Light Ale is the ordinary bitter carbonated, while Viking Pale Ale is the equivalent of the Best Bitter. They also brew Monarch, a barley wine, and a Stout and Brown Ale.

Morland's can be found at *The White Hart* in **Harwell**, an old partially half-timbered residential inn in the High Street, which serves full meals and snacks. A small pub at **Steventon**, which has Morland's beers straight from the barrel, is the *North Star*. The village is on the A34 about four miles south of Abingdon, and you find the pub by turning off the main road into the village. It is close to the church. There are several Morland pubs in **Reading** itself, a town which has quite a variety of beers, but is not, perhaps, worth a visit otherwise. At **Beedon** on the main north–south A34 is a simple roadside pub, *The Coach and Horses*, which has an excellent selection of hot and cold snacks. On Saturday and Sunday there is live music in the saloon bar, and you can play bar billiards in the public. In **Hungerford**, a quiet country town on the River Kennet, the *John O'Gaunt Inn*, on a corner at the bottom of the High Street, serves good ale. A free house, it serves Morland's bitter from the cask; a convenient halt if you are going to watch race-horses being trained on the Downs.

Another name to be seen in Berkshire is HENLEY ALES. Brewed by Brakspear's at Henley, this is very good beer, usually worth searching for. Brakspear pubs are found mainly in towns and villages along the Thames, especially between Maidenhead and Henley. On the A23 two miles south of **Hurley**, *The Red Lion* advertises itself, as you approach from Henley, as 'the last pub before London'. It is, admittedly, the last on this road before the motorway and is a cosy place to stop. On this same road at **Remenham** is *The Five Horse-shoes*, an attractive residential inn. Down the hill, still in Remenham, *The Two Brewers* is a pleasant little pub, just over the bridge from Henley and tucked away at a lower level than the London road, on the turning to Twyford. It does meals and snacks and is fairly smart but welcoming. Farther south, you can enjoy Henley Ales in **Twyford** at *The King's Arms* in the middle of the village and in **Wokingham** at *The Hope and Anchor*. In **Sandhurst**, just north of the A30 near Camberley, *The Wellington Arms* is another Henley Ales outpost.

Once across the Thames you enter Oxfordshire, and **Henley** is one of the country's brewing towns. The firm of W. H. BRAKSPEAR has been established in the centre of the town since 1779 and continues to brew excellent distinctive traditional beers. They include draught Pale Ale (ordinary bitter), SBA (special bitter) and draught mild. The Special Bitter is strong compared with most draught bitters available today and has a very full flavour. Brakspear also produce a Keg bitter (Beehive) and a range of bottled beers, of which Henley Strong Ale is worth trying.

Henley Brewery is fortunate to have pubs in some of the most charming villages in England, and many of their houses are fine examples of country buildings of different periods; some, such as *The Crooked Billet* (at **Stoke Row** in the Chiltern Hills to the west of the B481 road), date back to the 16th century. In **Henley** there are plenty of Brakspear houses, but one especially cosy little pub, next to the brewery in New Street, is *The Rose and Crown*. For those who may not want the well-kept ale straight out of the barrel, coffee is always available.

On the Henley–Oxford road, A423, Henley pubs abound. *The Fox* at **Bix**, just past the B480 turning to Watlington, is a thirties-style red-brick building, but very welcoming inside with a good selection of snacks, and tables and chairs in the garden. In the pretty village of **Nettlebed**, a comfortable country inn, *The White Hart* offers meals and accommodation, as well as good beer. Still on the A423, at the top of a hill near the turn-off to **Nuffield**, a simple old pub, *The Crown*, is an ideal stopping place, with a fine view to the west. The tiny bar has a large fireplace, and the back of the bar itself has ancient exposed beams in the roof. You will find sandwiches, a friendly welcome and Brakspear's ordinary bitter or Beehive Keg.

At **Goring-on-Thames**, south of Wallingford, *The Catherine Wheel*, which does meals, is well known locally for its warm welcome and the proprietors' enthusiasm for proper draught beer. Hard to find, it is in Station Road, which runs parallel to the High Street towards the railway. In the same attractive riverside town you can find Henley beer at *The John Barleycorn* near the river, and farther north, along the B4009, there is *The Perch and Pike* at **South Stoke**.

A particularly fine old thatched pub is *The Bottle and Glass*, near **Binfield Heath**, up a minor road some two miles west of **Shiplake**, on the Thames, where *The Plowden Arms* is a house of character. The blue Henley sign is to be seen outside the low partly-thatched *Six Bells* in **Warborough**, just two miles north of Shillingford on the Henley–Oxford road. Just to the east, only a few miles from the M40, lies the little town of **Watlington**, a quiet place with several welcoming pubs, including Brakspear's *The Fox and Hounds*, and Morland's *The Black Horse*. Three miles out of town to the east, at the junction of the B480 and B481 roads, stands *The Jolly Ploughman* at **Howe Hill**, a friendly country inn.

One Morland's pub easily missed in a lovely village is *The Shepherd's Hut* at **Ewelme**. The small church is one of the finest in the Chilterns, with a carved angel roof in one side chapel and a magnificent font cover. Near by is the 15th-century school building. After looking at the village, by-pass the Watney pub in the centre and find this unpretentious little house on the corner of a T junction at the edge of the village. It serves all three draught beers by handpump and does good sandwiches. To the south of Ewelme on the A423 at **Crowmarsh Gifford**, you can drink Morland's beer, under top pressure this time, at *The Bell*, a pleasant, comfortable pub.

One of the most interesting of the small towns along the Thames is **Dorchester**, whose history goes back over 1000 years. It was once the seat of a Bishopric and its medieval church looks imposing enough to be a cathedral. *The George Inn*, a former coaching inn on the main road opposite the church, has an inviting entrance to an old courtyard. The bar is low-beamed, large and dark with comfortable seats, and the beer is all it should be. There is also a pleasant restaurant, and rooms to let. You will find Morland's pubs, too, in **Henley**, in **Thame** (*The Star and Garter*), in the secluded old town of **Bampton**, south of Witney, with its magnificent stone houses and church, and also in **Oxford**.

Oxford has a brewery of its own, in the very centre of town. Morrell's Lion Brewery is in St Thomas Street, not far from Carfax. Brewing has been carried on at this site since the Middle Ages when Oseney Abbey was here. A family named Kenton leased the brewhouse early in the 18th century, and for the next 100 years their descendants maintained the brewing business. In 1803 Mark and James Morrell took over the lease, and from then a Morrell has been connected with the business. Today's chairman, Colonel

Morrell, is only the fifth generation in 170 years. The company remains small, with about 150 tied houses in the 30 miles around Oxford, but, like so many of the small independent brewers, they find that business is increasing as the public become more aware of the qualities of traditionally brewed beer.

Morrell's blue-and-white signs are easily found in **Oxford**, though gradually hand-painted pictorial inn-signs are replacing the simple name boards. *The Wheatsheaf*, near Carfax, off High Street, is one place to try Morrell's bitter, which is pale in colour but has a good hoppy flavour. Draught Light Ale is a kind of pale mild ale and Draught Varsity is a stronger bitter. There is also Varsity Keg Bitter and Pale Ale Keg, both brewed in the same way as the draught, but filtered and chilled to aid keeping qualities. The bottled Castle Ale has been a prizewinner at brewing shows, and College Ale is a good strong ale. *The Marlborough Arms* in St Thomas Street, next door to the brewery, is a pleasant local, with dartboard put to good use, and, above the bar, a display of objects connected with the brewery's history. One of them, a tap for a beer barrel, has an incredibly long neck. It was in use before the last war, when undergraduates of the university were not allowed to enter pubs. This tap protruded right through the wall beside a pub and 'scouts' or college servants each had their own key to draw off beer for the students.

Before leaving Oxford, you will find it rewarding to search for one of the most fascinating pubs in the city. *The Turf Tavern* is tucked away off New College Lane in St Helen's Passage and, apart from the attraction of the building and its position, is noteworthy in serving Hook Norton draught bitter. *The Turf Tavern* is a free house, but in the area north of Oxford you can find a number of pubs with the Hook Norton sign.

Outside the city, an attractive Morrell's pub is at **Iffley Lock**, just south of the suburb of Iffley; on the river bank, *The Isis* can be reached only on foot or by boat. Another pub in a pretty waterside situation is *The Boat* at **Thrupp** on the Oxford Canal, just off the A423 road east of Woodstock. You can drink Morrell's beers, too, at the *Rose and Crown* at **Woodstock**. It is on the northern edge of this glorious town built at the gates of Blenheim Palace. A more modern pub in a small village is *The Lamb and Flag* at **Longworth**. Just to the north of the A420 Faringdon–Oxford road, near Kingston Bagpuze, it is bright and welcoming, and has a steak bar. Just three miles west of Hinksey on the western Oxford by-pass is one of Morrell's most historic houses, *The Bear and Ragged Staff* at **Cumnor**. Built originally about 1360 as the farm-house to Cumnor Place, the inn was the scene of the murder of Amy Robsart, wife of the Earl of Leicester, 200 years later. Largely rebuilt in the 17th century, *The Bear and Ragged Staff* is well worth a detour, for its history, its beer and its food. Another historic pub, stone built with very old oak beams, serves Morrell's beer in the village of **Stanton Harcourt**, a few miles west of Cumnor on the B4449 to Eynsham. It is the *Harcourt Arms*, named after the family who were connected with the village for over 600 years.

Just off the re-aligned A40 between Witney and Oxford, but visible from the road, a little stone pub bears the Morrell sign. It is the *Britannia Inn* at **Barnard Gate**, near Eynsham. The draught beer is under pressure, but the welcome is good, and you can get sandwiches even on a Sunday evening

In Witney there is a Morrell house in Corn Street, which leads off the pleasant church green. The *Red Lion* is cosy and welcoming with well-used dark wooden stools and bar top.

HOOK NORTON BREWERY CO. is a fine example of a real old country brewery. Hook Norton is an attractive village in the northern Cotswolds, near Chipping Norton. Brewing began in 1849 in a farmhouse in the village, and at the turn of the century the present brewery was built. It is an imposing tower brewery, particularly set as it is at the end of a narrow lane on the edge of the village. The present proprietors, Bill Clarke and his son David, are respectively grandson and great grandson of the founder. Some of the twenty-six employees have been with the firm many years, and it remains a small, very personal company, brewing excellent beer, in basically the same way with the same machinery as at the opening of the brewery seventy-four years ago.

Hook Norton's brewing policy is dictated by the needs of the country area around. The most popular beer is a light bitter, and there is little demand for a more expensive strong bitter, so the company concentrates on Hook Norton Bitter and a pale mild ale, called Hookey, which is only faintly sweet. The same two beers, lightly carbonated, are bottled as Jackpot Ale and Hook Brown.

Most Hook Norton houses are quite simple village pubs, such as *The Three Conies* at **Thorpe Mandeville**, just north of Banbury on the B4525, and *The Pear Tree*, which is in **Hook Norton** itself, at the end of Brewery Lane. You can, however, try Hook Norton beer in some of the Cotswold towns, in **Banbury** at *The Reindeer Inn* in Parson Street, a very old pub, which has been carefully modernised, and in **Chipping Norton**, noted as Oxfordshire's highest town, at *The Red Lion*. **Woodstock**, too, has a minute Hook Norton house. *The Queen's Own* is a friendly, front-parlour pub on the main through road of the town, on the left going north. It is easy to miss, being in a terraced row of stone houses slightly above the road level, and without even a sign.

While in Woodstock, you might cross the road from the *Queen's Own* and try the bar of the comfortable hotel *The Marlborough Arms*. A free house, it serves a draught bitter from Wiltshire, made by WADWORTH'S OF DEVIZES. The bitter is under top pressure here, but it is worth trying, though to many people's taste it differs from the same brew served direct from the barrel or through a beer engine. Although Wadworth's are a Wiltshire brewer, they acquired some years ago the tiny brewery of GARNE'S in **Burford**, so you will see a few Wadworth houses in this area.

Garne's old brewery stands next to the *Lamb Inn* in Sheep Street. Used now partly as a storage depot, it has the word 'Brewery' cut in stone over the doorway. *The Lamb* is a perfect example of an old Cotswold hotel. There is a stone-flagged floor in the bar, which has a welcoming open fire in winter. The Wadworth's beer is served straight from the barrel and is first class. As there are also comfortable, modernised bedrooms, a cosy sitting-room and an excellent restaurant, it is well worth a detour to spend the night (book in advance!), or just to pass an hour in the old bar.

Also in this beautiful Cotswold town is another notable Wadworth pub. This is *The Royal Oak* in Witney Street, off the High Street. Simpler than *The Lamb*, it, too, is most welcoming, with a noisy locals' bar in the front and the saloon bar entered from the side street, where you can get good snacks. At **Witney** Wadworth's beer can be found in a small town pub, *The Griffin*, on the way out of town towards Oxford and, south of here, in the beautiful old town of **Bampton** at *The Jubilee*.

Travelling north-west from Burford along the high ridge

between the Evenlode and Windrush valleys, you cross the border into Gloucestershire, close to the village of **Fifield**, which is away from the main A424 on the right. By the turning to the village stands a lone building, *The Merrymouth Inn*. It looks rather bare, almost forbidding from the outside, but inside is a cosy, warm parlour with old, wooden tables and comfortable seats. The draught beer, ordinary or best bitter, is served by handpump and is undoubtedly a local brew. The beer comes from **Donnington Brewery**, only eight miles or so up the road past Stow on the Wold. It is a real country brewery, situated by a lake up a narrow lane near the village of Donnington. Run personally by Mr Claude Arkell, it has only fifteen employees and seventeen tied houses, but continues to prosper by virtue of its good distinctive beers.

In **Stow on the Wold** near by, famed for its large market square surrounded by mellow stone houses, you can drink Donnington Ales at *The Queen's Head*, an inconspicuous little pub at the northern end of the square. It is a simple clean place with one or two rooms to let, and you can drink your beer and eat sandwiches on benches outside in the square. It is a good place for draught cider too, if you want a change from beer.

Near **Stow** on the A436, which runs west towards Cheltenham, there is a particularly attractive Donnington house at **Lower Swell**, *The Golden Ball*. On the B4077 road to Tewkesbury a simple old country pub in a very secluded spot is *The Plough* at **Ford**. This is a few miles north of the village of **Guiting Power**, which once belonged to the Powers (or Poers) and stands on the River Guiting, now the Windrush. There is an interesting Norman church and stone cottages by the village green. You can also call in for a pint of Donnington beer at *The Farmer's Arms*.

Along the bottom of the steep western edge of the Cotswolds runs the main road from Cheltenham to Stratford, and overlooking it a number of small stone villages scramble up the side of the hill or perch on top. One of the loveliest, with its mellow walls and well-proportioned houses, is **Stanton**, just four or five miles south of Broadway. It is a pleasant stroll up the gently sloping village street to Donnington's *The Mount Inn*.

Before leaving the Cotswolds, **Moreton in Marsh** is a 'must', with its wide main street and fine buildings, including the medieval former jail tower. You can find Donnington beer here in *The Black Bear Inn*, and that other Cotswold beer, Hook Norton, can be enjoyed in *The Wellington*, on the Chipping Norton road just before the edge of town.

Gloucestershire was once the home of the Cheltenham and Hereford Brewery, whose trademark was 'West Country Beers'. The brewery in Cheltenham remains, but the beer brewed there is sold under the name of Whitbread. Many houses in the county still carry the sign 'West Country Beers' together with the Whitbread name, and in many of them the draught beer comes from Cheltenham. Usually their Trophy Bitter is locally brewed, as is PA (Pale Ale), which is to me half-way between a mild and a bitter and can be tasty if served by handpump.

In parts of Gloucestershire you can find Wadworth's beer from Devizes. At **Tewkesbury**, a picturesque town at the confluence of the Severn and Avon rivers, and in a wonderful position for river cruising, rowing or fishing, the Wadworth pub is *The Berkeley Arms* in Church Street. A few miles east of Tewkesbury, off the A435 to Evesham, is an attractive roadside pub at the turning to **Beckford**. *The Beckford Hotel* is one of the few pubs in the county to serve DAVEN-PORT'S beer. This brewery, which has won a number of prizes for its draught and bottled beer, is in Birmingham, but has a few tied houses in counties round about. At **Uley**, a small village near Dursley to the south of Stroud, *The King's Head*, a residential house, has Wadworth's beer, and you can also drink it at **Tetbury** at the oddly named *Trouble House*. In **Cheltenham**, a town with many striking 18th-century buildings, a tree-lined Promenade and, of course, the famous pump room, Wadworth's have *The Cotswold Hotel* (no longer residential) in Portland Street, a graceful, well-kept building.

In the south-eastern part of Gloucestershire, towards the Wiltshire border, another name appears on some pubs, Arkell's of Swindon. One place to try their beer is in **Ciren-cester**, at *The Golden Cross*, where you can have a lunchtime snack with your beer, after looking at the magnificent 15th-century church. At nearby **Fairford**, whose church's medieval stained glass became so well known during the local Concorde test flights, *The Bull Hotel* is a fine 200-year-old coaching inn in the Market Place. Farther east along the main road towards Faringdon, you can find Arkell's beer again at *The Red Lion* in **Lechlade**.

From here it is only some ten miles south to **Swindon**, a

bustling, mainly modern town, and in the northern outskirts you come to the village of **Upper Stratton**. Here stands the Kingsdown Brewery of J. ARKELL AND SONS LTD., and Arkell's is the most easily found local beer in and around Swindon. In the mid-19th century, with the railway which was to accelerate Swindon's growth into a large modern town under construction, Mr John Arkell founded his brewery, foreseeing the need of railway workers for plenty of beer. Since 1843—the same year as the launching of the SS *Great Britain*—the business has been in the same family, the present chairman being the fourth generation in direct line of descent. The present buildings, distinguished by the tall stone tower of the brewhouse, were built in 1861, although much modernised. Several fascinating old machines are still in use, such as a barrel filler, in beautifully polished brass and copper, which was bought in the 1930s from another brewer, but which is obviously Victorian in origin.

Arkell's brew two draught bitters, John Arkell Bitter and a best (BBB) as well as North Star keg bitter. The company decided some while ago to adopt only metal casks, because they are easier to keep clean, and they generally prefer the beer to be kept under a light covering of CO_2 to exclude air. Provided the landlord does not allow too much gas pressure in pumping the beer to the bar, flavour is not affected. The BBB is a pleasant, quite full-flavoured bitter, with a taste of hops, no doubt due to the dry hopping which is carried out in the brewery before despatch. Right opposite the brewery you can try the beer in its best condition at *The Wheatsheaf*. In Station Road, **Swindon**, *The Noah's Ark* is the modernised former Great Western Hotel, interestingly decorated with a railway theme, and with a comfortable restaurant. *The Baker's Arms*, Emlyn Square, in what is known as the Railway Village, is also worth a call. The *King's Arms Hotel*, Wood Street, in Swindon's Old Town, provides comfortable rooms as well as Arkell's beer. Outside the town, you can try Arkell's at *The Black Horse* in **Wanborough**, on the Roman Ermin Street just three miles north of junction 15 on the M4, or on the south side of the same motorway turn-off, at the simple *Baker's Arms*, **Badbury**. West from Swindon, in **Wootton Bassett** on the A420 road, the Arkell's sign is to be seen at *The Currier's Arms*.

Farther west on this road is **Sutton Benger**, at a turning to Captain Mark Phillips' village of Great Somerford. *The*

Wellesley Arms is a comfortable old pub which serves a good selection of snacks. It also serves a draught bitter of quite astonishing strength and mellowness called Old Timer. This ale, a prize-winning brew in 1972, is made by WADWORTHS in the market town of Devizes.

It was one century ago in 1875 that Mr Henry Wadworth bought a brewing business which had been in operation in Northgate Street since 1768. Within ten years business had grown so much that a new brewery was built near by, and today the tall red brick building stands on the site of the old Northgate of the town. Wadworths are proud of their traditional method of brewing and find by their success that it is popular. They use predominantly wooden casks for their draught beer, because they are convinced that the wooden barrels keep their beer well. They have their own cooper and will train another man when needed so that they can stick to beer from the wood. Their beers are racked straight into the casks, a few dry hops added to the bitter and finings added just before the casks leave the brewery. The company also likes its draught beer served without any CO_2 pressure, and encourages its pubs to use beer engines or to serve straight from the barrel. For those pubs which keep their barrels behind the bar, they have even devised a cooling jacket which maintains the beer at the right temperature, without direct refrigeration.

In **Devizes** it is easy to find Wadworth's pubs, but one of note is *The Bear Hotel* in the Market Place. It is a typical country town hotel, serving snacks and meals, as well as offering accommodation. Next to the brewery is *The White Lion* in Northgate Street, and in New Park Street another comfortable hotel is *The Castle*.

In the northern part of the county, where the east–west A4 road traverses the Downs, the country town of **Marlborough** is a good stopping place. In the wide main street there are one or two hotels, but one small inn on the south side of the street which you could easily miss is Wadworth's *The Green Dragon*. It's a friendly 'locals' pub, which serves sandwiches and snacks. Marlborough is only a few miles east of **Avebury**, a village famous because of its situation, built partly across a large prehistoric stone circle and ditch. Close by is *The Waggon and Horses* at **Beckhampton** on the A4. At **Aldborne**, north-east of Marlborough, only a few miles from the M4, *The Blue Boar*'s attractive pictorial sign beckons you into a pleasant pub, and to the south of Marlborough lies **Pewsey**, where *The French Horn* is well situated close to the Kennet and Avon Canal.

In or near most of the Wiltshire country towns there is a Wadworth house, such as *The King's Arms*, which offers accommodation in **Melksham**, midway between Devizes and Bath. *The Lamb* at **Trowbridge** is a comfortable inn, in a town where Ushers used to brew their Wiltshire beer until taken over by the Watney giant. Brewing is still carried on here, but in a different tradition, and Watneys are said to be due to close the brewery. Farther south, near the Dorset border, a most comfortable, historic inn in a delightful small village is *The Seymour Arms* at **East Knoyle**. The village is found on the A350 to Shaftesbury, and near by is another pub with historic associations, *The Beckford Arms* in **Fonthill Gifford**, named after the 18th-century writer William Beckford, who built the Gothic edifice of Fonthill Abbey.

The cathedral city of **Salisbury** still has its own local brewery. GIBBS, MEW AND CO. is a family company which has been in operation for five generations. The Anchor Brewery has been in operation for over 200 years. The name Anchor Keg, given to the strongest of the firm's keg beers, commemorates the brewery name.

Gibbs ceased to produce traditional draught bitter several years ago and concentrate now on their three keg bitters, Special PA, the weakest, Blue Keg and Anchor. They do, however, brew a more traditional Mild, which is usually dispensed by top pressure. Of their bottled beers, one to note is Sarum Special, a quite strong pale ale.

In the heart of 'Gibbsland' around Salisbury, there are plenty of their blue-and-white signs. In **Salisbury** city there are no less than eleven Gibbs houses, the nearest to the cathedral being *The Bell and Crown* in Catherine Street. In the old town of **Amesbury**, the nearest town to Stonehenge, *The George Hotel* is a pleasant place to stop. Another, simpler, Gibbs house near by is *The Bell* at **Winterbourne Stoke**, on the A303 west of Stonehenge. A delightful pub beside the River Wylye, four miles north of Wilton, is *The Swan Inn* at **Stoford**, where hot and cold snacks can be eaten in the riverside garden. A historic pub in a small village is the 15th-century *King's Arms* at **Downton**, on the B3080 about seven miles south of Salisbury. A welcoming Gibbs inn, which has a small restaurant, is *The Yew Tree* at **Odstock** just two miles into the country south from Salisbury.

Another name to be seen in Salisbury and to the west along the Dorset border is that of HALL AND WOODHOUSE, whose Badger Beers are brewed in Dorset at Blandford. The *New Inn* is in New Street near the cathedral.

WK

Jennings' Castle Brewery, Cockermouth, Cumbria (p. 94)

The Donnington Brewery,
near Stow-on-the-Wold,
Gloucestershire (p. 43)

Belhaven Brewery,
Dunbar, Scotland (p. 105)

The yeast head being skimmed at Theakston's Brewery, Masham, Yorkshire. Another head will form after this, which is left as a protective blanket over the wort—or beer as it is now—until the vessel is emptied (p. 94)

The cooper's shop at Wadworth's Northgate Brewery, Devizes, Wilts (p. 46)

MORRELL'S TRUSTEES
LION BREWERY
OXFORD

⚛ HUNTING AND ⚛

Cycling Road Map

OF

OXFORD

AND DISTRICT.

(SCALE 1 MILE TO ¼ INCH)

WITH LIST OF HOTELS AND INNS WITHIN EASY RIDING DISTANCE FROM OXFORD, WHERE **MORRELL'S TRUSTEES'** CELEBRATED ALES AND STOUT MAY BE OBTAINED, ALSO REFRESHMENTS AT THE CYCLIST CLUB TARIFF.

Over fifty years ago brewers were offering maps to their customers. Morrell's still brew at the Lion Brewery Oxford, but their prices have increased since those days!

The Swan Inn, Southwold, Suffolk (p. 120)

The Bear and Ragged Staff, Cumnor, Oxfordshire (p. 41)

Drays and draught horses at
Adnam's Brewery, Southwold,
Suffolk (p. 115)

Pulling a pint of Young's in
The Crane, Wandsworth, South
London (p. 14)

The George, Norton St. Philip,
Somerset, a historic Wadworth
pub (p. 55)

The Plough, Leigh, Surrey, one
of King and Barnes' houses
(p. 26)

The Sea Horse with its garden,
Shalford, near Guildford,
Surrey (p. 25)

Buckley's *The Beach Hotel*, Pendine, South Wales (p. 84)

The Red Lion, Chalton, Hampshire, a Gale's house (p. 34)

The Nutshell, The Traverse, Bury St Edmunds, Suffolk. Greene King's—and Britain's—smallest pub (p. 116)

The Red Lion, a common inn name, was the emblem of John of Gaunt. This one is at Boldre, near Lymington, Hampshire (p. 35)

The Shipwright's Arms, a Devenish inn in Helford, Cornwall (p. 63)

A small selection of the many different beer labels in use

The West Country
Dorset, Somerset, Avon, Devon, Cornwall

Often neglected by holiday-makers, hastening to Devon and Cornwall, *Dorset* has much to offer. In Thomas Hardy's Wessex grassy chalk downlands in the north and west give way in the east to flatter heath land towards the edge of the New Forest. The coast has some of the country's most attractive resorts in Lyme Regis, Weymouth and Swanage, and everywhere are delightful villages, often of low, thatch-roofed houses. The towns are small, with a country-market air, and almost all have retained much of the appearance they had a century or more ago.

Dorset, in beer terms, is also remarkable for such a small county in still having four independent brewery companies. All four are in a very healthy state and report increasing sales of their varied, distinctive Dorset beers.

Coming from the east the name most likely to be seen first is that of HALL AND WOODHOUSE, who brew their Badger Beers in **Blandford Forum**. They have a number of pubs all over the county, as well as in the west of Hampshire. Blandford is a town of predominantly 18th-century red-brick buildings. The Market Place is especially fine, having been rebuilt after a fire in the 18th century. The church, which dominates the Market Place, is an excellent example of the renaissance style.

Hall and Woodhouse have been established since the late 18th century, though their present brewery dates from 1882. The Victorian red-brick building is just across the River Stour at **Blandford St Mary,** a few yards up the road to Poole. The nearest place in which to try Badger beer is *The Stour Inn,* a snug little pub, on a small green close to Blandford Bridge. Here they serve the bitter through a beer engine, which is becoming unusual, as many Badger houses are switching to a top-pressure system.

In **Blandford Forum** one of the leading hotels, *The Crown*, is a Badger house. It is a large brick building near the river and round the corner from the Market Place. It has a comfortable lounge and dining-room, as well as a large fairly smart bar, which seems to be a meeting place for locals as well as visitors. Almost next door the attractive sign of *The Three Choughs* is found over the door of an equally attractive old pub, which has been modernised inside, but retains its old beams. Two minutes walk up Salisbury Street from the Market Place brings you to a cross-roads, and on the opposite corner is a fairly plain, square building, but with the usual tasteful symmetry of the late 18th century. It is *The Badger Hotel*, really a local pub with rooms, and offering a friendly welcome from the young landlord and his wife. Best Bitter as well as ordinary and Forum Keg bitter is available.

Before leaving Blandford, try for comparison Gibbs Mew's beer in *The White Hart* in East Street, the only other provincial beer in town, though it is keg or bottled only.

To the north and east of Blandford, you can find Badger beers at *The Roebuck* in the quaintly named village of **Six-penny Handley** on the A354 and at the *Bugle Horn* at **Tarrant Gunville**, just off the same road about six miles north of Blandford. This is the lovely area of Cranborne Chase, and its winding lanes are worth exploring. It is bounded on the west by the Shaftesbury–Blandford road, and on this road the village of **Fontmell Magna** is particularly pretty. Some of the film of *Tom Jones* was shot here. The village pub is *The Crown*, a Badger house.

Shaftesbury is a fine old town high on a hill with glorious views over Blackmoor Vale to the south. Most of the pubs in town have the Hall and Woodhouse sign; they are mostly small local taverns, except for *The Crown* in the High Street, a comfortable hotel, *The Ship*, just off New Road, and *The King's Arms*, in Bleake Street. In Shaftesbury *The Mitre Inn* has the jolly huntsman sign of Eldridge Pope's beer, brewed in Dorchester. In this area of north Dorset, however, Badger pubs predominate, partly due to Hall and Woodhouse's acquisition several years ago of Matthew's brewery in **Gillingham**, a little town about five miles along the B3081, north of Shaftesbury. *The Phoenix Inn* in the town provides tasty Badger beer. South of here in Blackmoor Vale lies **Sturminster Newton**, which has a fine old stone bridge over the Stour and several attractive pubs, notably Hall and Woodhouse's *The Bull Inn* on the south side, which boasts a skittle alley. At **Buckland Newton**, a pretty village some ten miles south on the edge of the downs, you will find *The Royal Oak*, and on the main Sturminster–Sherbourne road, a pleasant roadside pub, *The White Hart*, at **Bishop's Caundle.**

Sherborne is at the extreme northern edge of Dorset, home of the famous public school and with a splendid medieval church. *The Britannia Inn* in Westbury Street is itself a historic building, over 200 years old, formerly a school; it provides meals and snacks, lets rooms, has a skittle alley and serves excellent Hall and Woodhouse bitter and mild. Another residential house is *The Antelope* in Greenhill. You can also find Eldridge Pope's Huntsman Ales in the town in several of the hotels, including *The Black Horse.*

Dorchester, the most attractive and historic county town with its main street running down a long hill to the bridge over the River Frome, is the home of ELDRIDGE POPE AND Co., whose brewery near the railway was built in 1880. Mr Charles Eldridge in fact acquired his first brewery some forty-five years before this, and beer has been brewed in Dorchester for over 300 years. Eldridge Pope's brew a wide range of beer, including two draught milds, notably XXXX, which has been a show prizewinner as a strong mild ale, and three draught bitters. The strongest bitter, IPA, won prizes in 1960, and again in 1972. These are well-flavoured traditional beers, usually served in pubs by a top-pressure system. Among their bottled beers, Green Top Pale Ale has regularly won prizes, while in 1968 the company brewed a special ale for the Hardy Festival. Called Thomas Hardy's Ale, it is claimed to be the strongest ale in Britain and to be keepable for up to twenty-five years. It is luckily still to be bought in local pubs and off licences—but only in nips!

The Huntsman Ales trademark is to be seen in a wide area around Dorchester. In Dorchester itself, where there seems to be a pub every few yards, there are fourteen Eldridge Pope houses. One worth visiting is near Hardy's old home, Max Gate, and is named *The Trumpet Major*, after the novel. It is in Wareham Road. Another pub with a history is *Goldie's Bars* in High East Street. Named after a former wine merchant of the town, it is close to Eldridge Pope's old brewery. An archway a few doors downhill proclaims 'Pale Ale Brewery'. In a town with so many pubs, you can find other local Dorset beers, such as those of Hall and Woodhouse, in *The White Hart Hotel* in High East Street. The Weymouth beer brewed by DEVENISH AND Co. is also to be found in the town; especially worth visiting is *The King's Arms* in High East Street. An historic coaching inn, it has associations with George III and Nelson and is a fine building, as well as a comfortable hotel. The little *Plume of Feathers* in Princes Street is also a pleasant Devenish pub.

In the country north of Dorchester the village of **Cerne Abbas** on the Sherborne road is quiet and full of lovely old houses, especially along Church Street. Near by is the famous hill figure of The Cerne Giant. *The New Inn* bears the Huntsman Ale sign and is a welcome spot for a fine meal or to spend the night, if you want to explore. Devenish's *The Royal Oak* is a good alternative.

Father east at **Piddletrenthide**, Eldridge Pope have *The European Inn*, an unspoiled pub with a lovely view from its garden, and Devenish *The Green Dragon*. **Puddletown** is noted for the beautiful village church of St Mary with its musician's gallery, for Dorset was one of the last places to keep to a band rather than adopting a church organ. The *Prince of Wales* here is a comfortable, welcoming inn, with an inglenook fireplace in the public bar. There is Badger bitter (on pressure), shove halfpenny and darts.

A remote village some eight miles north, off the main road near Winterborne Whitchurch, is **Milton Abbey**. It is worth a detour, for it is an example of 18th-century town planning. On each side of the main street are delightful pairs of 200-year-old thatched cottages. An 18th-century lord of the manor had the whole village rebuilt to his own plan. *The Hambro Arms* is a nice place to call in for a drink of Devenish ale too.

At the eastern edge of the county, **Wimborne Minster** is, as its name suggests, a town built round a great church. This is mainly Hall and Woodhouse land, and you can drink Badger beer in *The Dorset House Inn* in Church Street, where you may find fresh crab sandwiches, or, in the same street, *Oddfellows Arms*. Huntsman Ales are available in *The White Hart*, which is a residential inn, and Devenish's in *The Cricketer's Arms* in Park Lane. Not far to the west of here, Devenish Ales are to be found at *The Coventry Arms*, an attractive inn in the pretty village of **Corfe Mullen**.

Poole, an old town which has developed into a holiday resort like the more modern Bournemouth, still has some interesting areas, particularly round the harbour and the

Guildhall, you will find Devenish beer at *The Guildhall Tavern* in Market Street; Eldridge Pope beer is also available in the town, as at the *Pure Drop Inn*.

Among **Bournemouth**'s many fine hotels, one worth trying for local beer is Eldridge Pope's *South Western* by the Central Station. A two-star hotel, it recently won four regional catering awards, including 'chef of the year'.

In the Isle of Purbeck, Whitbread signs—the draught beer is often from Romsey—predominate, but Devenish have *The Scott Arms* at **Kingston Matravers**, which is up on a hill overlooking historic Corfe Castle, and in **Swanage** you should look for *The Mowlen*, which serves Hall and Woodhouse beer and has lobster salads, in season.

Weymouth, Dorset's largest seaside town, also has a pretty harbour whence ferry services run to the Channel Islands. That it has long been a brewing town is attested by the large number of pubs. There remains one brewery in the town, DEVENISH WEYMOUTH BREWERY. The brewery was founded in 1742 and became Devenish's in 1824, since when the brewing of Dorset ales has continued, even during the Second World War, when much of the brewery was bombed. When Devenish acquired the Weymouth brewing company of Groves some years ago, they also acquired Groves' pubs, which explains why you will find the Devenish heraldic dragon sign on fifty pubs and inns in Weymouth alone. One not to miss is *The Black Dog* in St Mary Street, a very old pub, at one time known as 'Dove Ale House' and supposedly a smugglers' haunt. On the Quay, *The Sailor's Return* is another pub where you can try a pint of Wessex IPA, which is Devenish's best bitter, or Saxon, a keg bitter.

There are other regional brews to be found in Weymouth, if you want a variation. Several hotels are Eldridge Pope houses, including *The Queen's Hotel*, and you can drink their Huntsman Ales in a few smaller pubs, such as *The Market House Tavern*. Hall and Woodhouse's Blandford beers are also represented in *The Portland Railway Hotel* in King Street.

In **Portland**, south of Weymouth, Devenish pubs are plentiful. The *George Inn* at **Reforne** is supposed to be the oldest house on the Isle of Portland. Along the coast to the east is beautiful Lulworth Cove. The nearest hamlet is **West Lulworth**, where *The Castle*, a little old thatched inn, is perfect for its position.

West of Weymouth *The Elm Tree Inn* is an attractive old country pub in **Langton Herring** near the sea opposite Chesil Bank, while at **Abbotsbury**, a village known for its swannery, Devenish have *The Ilchester Arms*, an old coaching inn.

Westwards from Abbotsbury, you will find the name PALMER'S outside a number of small country inns.

Bridport is the centre of Palmer's territory, for their brewery is situated on the south side of the town on the road to West Bay. An attractive old building, it is the only thatch-roofed brewery still operating and they also have a very old water wheel still working. Old letter books show that the brewery was in existence in 1794, becoming J C and R H Palmer at the turn of this century. The grandson of Mr J C Palmer is now the proprietor. Palmer's brew two draught beers, a bitter and best bitter, known as IPA. The same beers, lightly carbonated, are also bottled, as well as a brown, a stout and a strong ale. In most pubs the draught beer is served direct from the barrel or by handpump.

In **Bridport** itself you can try their beer at *The Swan Hotel* in West Street or *The Crown* in West Bay Road. The *Old Greyhound Hotel* in the centre of town in East Street is a Devenish house. At **West Bay** *The Bridport Arms* is a plain but comfortable one-star AA hotel near the harbour serving good Palmer's beers.

There are several picturesque village pubs in the rolling country north of Bridport, often with rooms for the night and ideal for a quiet stay. Many are Palmer's houses, including *The Crown* at **Uploders**, a pretty stone-built inn, just north of the A35 three miles out of Bridport. *The Farmer's Arms* at nearby **Loders** is an ordinary-looking pub in a charming village. If you take some really narrow lanes northwards from Loders, in about four miles you will come to **Powerstock**. It straggles up and down hill, and high above most of the village is the church with some interesting monuments. Just along the road *The Three Horseshoes* stands on a high point, with views from its garden down two valleys. It is a small inn, rather bare looking red-brick, but well decorated within with nets and other impedimenta to give it a sea-fishing atmosphere, not overdone. There are three rooms to let and snacks are available.

Seven miles north of Bridport, at the little town of **Beaminster**, you can get Palmer's Ales in *The Greyhound* in

The Square, while on the A35 between Bridport and Lyme Regis, a good place to stop is *The George Inn* at **Chideock**, which has accommodation and does evening meals and snacks. **Lyme Regis** on the Devon border is a delightful watering place, with attractive 18th-century houses. Two Palmer's houses are *Cobb Arms Hotel* on the Cobb to the west of the town and *The Pilot Boat* in Broad Street.

In Somerset and Avon pubs with local beer are pretty sparse, as no independent breweries survive in these counties. In the north some Courage houses will be serving draught beer brewed in Bristol, but it is not particularly distinctive. Similarly Whitbread supply some of their pubs with draught beer from Cheltenham. Otherwise it is best to look out for signs of the various Dorset brewers or Wadworths of Devizes.

Just over the border from Dorset, **Crewkerne** offers a variety of brews, with the residential *Swan Hotel* serving Devenish's, Eldridge Pope's Huntsman Ales available in *The White Hart Inn* and Palmer's Ales in *The Queen's Hotel*, Station Road.

North-west of Crewkerne, at **East Chinnock** on the A30 road, Eldridge Pope's Ales are to be found in *The Portman Arms*. Eldridge Pope beer is also served in several places in **Yeovil**, including the residential *Three Choughs Hotel*, and a few miles along the road to Castle Cary you can drink it in the *Red Lion* in **Marston Magna**.

Wincanton is a place to find Hall and Woodhouse pubs; the quaintly named *Nog Inn* in the High Street does snacks and lets rooms. At the village of **Holton**, west along the A303, *The Old Inn* is also a Badger house, and, east of the town, a turn north off the A303 at Burton brings you to **Penselwood** and *The Queen's Head*, which is only a few miles from the stately home of Stourhead. If you are seeking local ale on the road from Shepton Mallet to Ilchester, the Roman Fosse Way, look for the Eldridge Pope sign at **Lydford on Fosse**, on the *Lydford Hotel*. *The Theobald Arms* at **Nunney** on the A359 three miles south-west of Frome is worth visiting for Hall and Woodhouse beer. North in what is now Avon, around Bath and the southern fringes of Bristol, a few Wadworth's pubs are to be found. In particular, at the attractive village of **Norton St Philip** between Bath and Frome the historic *George Inn* offers a friendly welcome. The building itself is striking; the ground floor with a porch is stone, while above it are two storeys of Elizabethan half-timbering. The Wadworth Wiltshire bitter is served by handpump. At *The Red Lion*, a pleasant 18th-century house in **Woolverton** just three miles south from here along the B3110, it is served by gravity direct from the cask.

Bath itself cannot, of course, be described in a few words. But to those visiting the city who are interested in beer as well as in history, architecture and art, Bath can offer some pubs which serve local beer. Among them is *The Cœur de Lion*, an old inn wedged among the shops in Northumberland Passage. It is one of a fairly small number of pubs which serve Devenish bitter through a beer engine. In Cleveland Place West the plain-looking but friendly *Curfew Inn* keeps Wadworth beers. Gibbs' Salisbury beer is available in Bath at *The Angel Hotel* in Eastgate Street, which has a large restaurant.

Bristol has little distinctive local beer. Courage's draught is brewed in the city in the former George's Brewery, so Courage pubs are frequent. However Davenport's ales can be drunk at the rather bare *Bay Horse* in Lewins Mead, while another rather ordinary pub, *The Phoenix* in Wellington Road, offers Wadworth's.

Between Bristol and Cheddar and the Mendips the main road runs over some lower hills and just two miles off it, in **Winford**, *The Crown Inn* is a good place to drink Wadworth's beer; or, farther along this road, try *The Bungalow Inn* at **Redhill**.

You can find the same beer at **Blagdon**, a village on the A368, which runs along beside the northern edge of the Mendips. Here *The New Inn* has accommodation and is well placed for exploring the hills. *The Miner's Arms* at **Priddy** sounds like a pub, but is in fact a licensed restaurant without a bar as such, but mentioned here because the proprietor has recently taken to brewing his own beer. It is reportedly good strong ale naturally conditioned in the bottle.

Bristol's seaside resort of **Clevedon** offers the chance of drinking Hall and Woodhouse beer at *The Regent Hotel*. It is not residential, but has meals and snacks.

South along the coast, it is hard to find distinctive beer in **Weston super Mare**, but a short trip to **Kewstoke** on the northern edge of the town close to the sea and to Weston Woods will bring you to *The Long John Silver*, which has Wadworth's excellent Devizes beer.

The rest of Somerset and Avon is left to the national brewers, though you may find regional beers in some free houses. *The Lamb Inn* at **Upton Noble**, a little old pub in a pleasant village on the A359 between Frome and Bruton, for instance, has Wadworth's draught 6X Strong Bitter; and in **Castle Cary**, farther south, a fascinating town of steep streets and ancient houses, *The Clarence Inn*, a small one-bar pub, sells all Wadworth's beers.

Devon is, like Somerset, a famous cider county, though sadly a large number of pubs now refuse to stock the excellent draught cider. It is also a county which has lost nearly all its locally brewed beers, but there is good beer to be found, if you search for it.

Only a few years ago, the national Courage group took over the last remaining independent brewer in the county, Plymouth Breweries. Courage have kept on the brewery, and the Plymouth Breweries (PB) sign is still displayed on a number of pubs. The draught mild and bitter may be brewed in Plymouth, but it will not differ greatly from draught Courage brewed in other places, and more often than not will be dispensed by CO_2 pressure. When in a Courage house have a good look to see if there is a handpump in use before accepting Tavern Keg.

The other brewery in Devon is at **Tiverton**, some fifteen miles north of Exeter, where Whitbread now control what used to be Starkey, Knight and Ford's pubs. Their beer was formerly advertised as 'Tivvy Ales'.

The locally brewed draught is available in most Whitbread houses in Devon under the general names of Trophy bitter and PA (mild, but not as sweet and thin as the dark mild of the south-east). The old name still exists in the bottled Tivvy Brown Ale.

In and around Exeter you may notice the name Heavitree outside some pubs. Heavitree's used to brew their own beer, but stopped doing so some time ago, and now simply own a number of houses. They sell almost exclusively Whitbread beers.

Apart from these two common signs, most of the other national brews can be found in Devon, including Bass-Worthington. The traditional draught version of this Burton-brewed beer is usually worth looking for, as in *The Great Western Hotel*, by St David's Station in **Exeter**. Surprising to find this in a Trust House Forte hotel.

You can find beer brewed by an independent brewer in nearby Dorset in **Exeter** and much of eastern Devon.

Devenish of Weymouth have a modern pub in the city centre, *The Valiant Soldier*, rather lush and serving good food, and a simpler pub in Blackboy Road, *The Ropemaker's Arms*. At **Ide**, just two miles out of Exeter to the south-west, off the A30 road, Devenish's *Huntsman Inn* is an attractive thatched pub, and on the road south to Dawlish, *The Royal Oak* at **Exminster** is a pleasant place to stop.

On the other side of the Exe estuary at **Topsham**, *The Bridge Inn* is a free house which serves Wadworth's Wiltshire beers, while you can find Devenish beers farther down on the coast at **Exmouth** in *The Bicton Inn* in Bicton Street, and in *Builder's Arms*, Princes Street. At **Withycombe Raleigh**, just on the north-east of Exmouth, Devenish beer can be drunk in *The Holly Tree Inn*, a useful place for snacks, and a night halt.

To the east along the coast, Devenish pubs can be easily found around **Sidmouth**. In the town on the Esplanade, the bar of the *Marine Hotel* serves an excellent pint of draught IPA, their best bitter. *The Bowd Inn* at **Bowd**, two miles north of Sidmouth on the main A3052 from Exeter, is another delightful Devon inn. Between Sidmouth and Budleigh Salterton, *The King's Arms* at **Otterton** has a caravan site attached.

At **Ottery St Mary**, also in the valley of the River Otter, the leading hotel, *King's Arms*, is a Devenish house. Only a few miles from here on the north side of the A30 is **Whimple**, noted for many years as the home of Whiteways Devon Cider. If, however, you want to stick to beer in this apple-growing district, Devenish's *New Fountain Inn* is in the High Street.

The A30 trunk road now happily by-passes **Honiton**, which makes it more peaceful if you want to spend the night; *The White Lion* in Mill Street has accommodation as well as Devenish's beer.

Farther east you can drink it in **Axmouth**, at *The Ship Inn*, and north of here, near Axminster, in the little village of **Hawkchurch**, near the Dorset border, where *The Old Inn* is worth a visit.

In this area can be found one of the West Country's most distinctive beers, brewed at Bridport, Dorset, by the small firm of Palmer's. Their excellent draught bitter is available at *Axminster Inn* in Church Street, **Axminster**, and at *The Millwey*, Chard Road, on the northern edge of town. At

Kilmington, just two miles west of Axminster, *The New Inn* is also a Palmer's house.

At **Kingsbridge**, north of Salcombe, an oasis for beer drinkers is *The King's Arms*, a free house which keeps Wadworth's excellent Wiltshire beer. This beer is also on sale east of here at **Slapton**, near sandy Start Bay, at the *Tower Inn*.

Some free houses in the north of the county have St Austell's beer from Cornwall, and in **Barnstaple** there are several Devenish pubs, such as *The Golden Lion Tap* in The Square and *Golden Fleece Hotel*, Tuly Street.

Elsewhere in Devon whole villages are sometimes the complete preserve of one brewer. In **Ashburton**, for instance, an attractive old town, with a very striking church tower, every pub serves Whitbread.

Crossing the River Tamar in Plymouth, you enter almost another country, *Cornwall*. Favoured with a mild, moist climate where tropical plants can grow, many miles of coastline with glorious cliffs, tiny harbours and fishing villages full of character, Cornwall is not surprisingly, perhaps Britain's favourite holiday area. The Duchy has suffered as well as prospered because of this, with its few and narrow roads clogged with cars and caravans and its towns crammed with visitors, who nevertheless provide a large proportion of the population with their living. Despite its popularity, Cornwall has preserved its character, and it is still possible to enjoy the coves and cliffs, wandering round little old towns like Helston and Fowey and drinking in historic old village inns. Cornwall is, of course, another great producer of cider, but the Cornishman also likes his beer, and there is still Cornish beer which certainly deserves attention.

St Austell is one of Cornwall's larger towns, set in the middle of the industrial area of the china clay mines and a mile or two from the south coast. The town has the older of the only two remaining breweries in the Duchy. The ST AUSTELL BREWERY, built in the traditional tower style, stands on a hill about the town. It dates from 1890, a boom time in brewery construction, but the company started some time earlier, in 1851, and is still controlled by the same family. St Austell pubs are to be found all over Cornwall, though there are more of them in the south and west. An ordinary and a best draught bitter are brewed, neither especially strong, but with a good full flavour. Bill Clarke, whose brewery at Hook Norton, Oxfordshire, makes its own excellent traditional bitter, says that St Austell's bitter is the nearest he has found to his own brew. There is also a St Austell mild and a keg bitter, which is not pasteurised, a process which, some people think, tends to give the beer a sweetish taste. In fact, St Austell are proud of the fact that none of their beers are pasteurised, and continue to mature in bottle or keg. In the town you might try the St Austell beer in *The Sun Inn*, a popular pub in Market Street where you find a warm welcome from Mr Harvey.

Some twenty miles farther west from St Austell along the A390, passing the cathedral city of Truro, lies another busy industrial town, the tin-mining centre of **Redruth**. It is here that DEVENISH, who began in Dorset and still brew there, have their second brewery. It is the most westerly of Britain's breweries. It seems that early in this century Major Devenish used to come down to Cornwall from Weymouth to go sailing and decided to try selling his beer. So successful was he that he bought two pubs in Falmouth and eventually acquired the Falmouth Brewery. Mallets Brewery in Truro was bought later, and in 1934 the Redruth Brewery, which is now Devenish's Cornish headquarters.

Apparently in the years after the First World War the beer was brought from Falmouth to Truro by barge and unloaded into the Mansion House cellars. The barge used to be moored where nowadays people park their cars outside Devenish's Lemon Quay off-licence. But these to my mind more interesting ways of delivering beer have now gone, and Devenish brew in Redruth only in Cornwall. They make the same range of beers as in Weymouth; draught bitter, and IPA (slightly stronger), draught mild, keg mild (Dark Keg) and keg bitter (Saxon). An interesting place to try these in Redruth itself is *The Red Lion*, a pub which is recommended for snacks and, if you don't already know, you will soon realise that Redruth is also in the heart of Cornish rugger country, when you see the landlord's collection of rugby caricatures. But as you would expect, there is no shortage of Devenish pubs in Redruth and around. To find St Austell beer you have to go out of Redruth about a mile along the A30 to Illogan highway to *The Railway Inn*.

Entering the county over the Tamar Bridge, the first sea-side place of interest you come to is **Looe**, which is reached by turning from the A38 on to the A387 southwards. Consisting of two parts, East and West Looe, which face each other across the bay, Looe is an historic fishing port, now rather crowded and full of 'Cornish pisky' shops, but still with much character; the 16th-century Guildhall is now a museum. St Austell beer should be looked for here. It is to be had in *The Ship Hotel* or the popular *Double Decker Bars*. Northwards, inland, is **Liskeard**, a fairly ordinary grey stone town, but a good base for exploring the southern part of Bodmin Moor. There is one St Austell pub here, the tiny *Barley Sheaf*, and Devenish's beer is also available, in *The Railway*.

Lostwithiel is a charming, quiet town, tucked away down sunken roads on the River Fowey, yet it has a station on the main London–Penzance railway line; a station which, when I last saw it, had a palm tree on the platform. There are several simple but cosy pubs in the town, notably *The King's Arms*, an old rambling inn which serves St Austell beers. *The Globe Inn* is another St Austell pub, while *The Monmouth Hotel*, a residential house which serves snacks, has Devenish's ales.

Fowey, south by a most attractive road along the Fowey estuary, is a delightful town of narrow streets and old houses, but with the bustle of a busy port from where china clay is shipped. This was 'Troy' in Quiller Couch's novel *Troy Town*. St Austell beer can be drunk in *The Riverside Hotel* and *The Lugger*. A trip by ferry across to **Polruan** brings you to *The Russell Inn*, another residential St Austell house.

Just about two miles north of Lostwithiel is the 12th-century Restormel Castle. Standing on the side of a hill, overlooking the valley, it looks from a distance like a set for a Walt Disney film.

Farther along on the road towards Bodmin, Lanhydrock House should also be visited. The late Tudor house, heavily restored in the same style in the last century, stands in a beautiful wooded park. It belongs to the National Trust. From here it is only three miles into **Bodmin**, the county town, which has little architectural distinction, except for St Petroc's church, the largest parish church in Cornwall, with some fine 15th-century work. The pubs are mainly small friendly locals, such as *The Barley Sheaf* and *The George and Dragon*, both St Austell houses. You can, however, drink Devenish's in *The Duke of Cornwall*, a plain but comfortable hotel in the middle of town.

To the east and north of Bodmin stretches lonely Bodmin Moor with a few isolated villages. The main A30 runs across the moor towards Launceston, and at Tregadillet, just before you reach the town, you find *The Eliot Arms*, Square and Compass, an old world inn which serves Devenish's beer.

The north coast of Cornwall is wilder and rockier than the south, with such striking coves as Crackington Haven (a really steep road runs down to the sea about three miles off the main A39) and Boscastle. The area is something of a desert for the discriminating beer drinker, with one St Austell house at Bude, *The Globe Hotel*, and the next seventeen miles south at Camelford, where *The Darlington Hotel* and *The Mason's Arms* both have this tasty beer. Not far away is Tintagel, where the so-called King Arthur's Castle is poised high above the sea. The nearest St Austell pub is in the slate-quarrying village of Delabole about four miles south on the B3314. The pub's name, *Bettle and Chisel*, is a reminder of the area's main occupation.

Travelling south-west along the A39 towards Wadebridge, a right turn down a small road about four miles before you reach the town takes you to St Kew, where the *St Kew Inn* is a very cosy 15th-century pub serving St Austell beer. In Wadebridge a St Austell house to visit is *The Swan Hotel*. On the coast near by is the old port and holiday resort of Padstow, where the Padstow hobby-horse dance takes place each spring. *The Harbour Inn* serves a good pint of St Austell bitter straight from the cask, or, if you prefer Devenish's Redruth ales, go to the *Golden Lion*, a plain-looking but pleasant residential inn.

As you move farther west the frequency of Devenish pubs increases, and there is one to be found in most towns and villages. In Newquay, noted for its beaches, *The Red Lion Hotel* is a fairly lush place with a fine view over the sea, and it has a comfortable restaurant. *Victoria Bars* is a popular place to drink St Austell's ales.

Truro is Cornwall's cathedral city (19th-century gothic) and is almost mid-way between north and south coasts. The river runs through the city making it possible to take a water-borne trip to Falmouth. *The Market Inn*, Lemon Quay, and *The Barley Sheaf*, Old Bridge Street, both offer Devenish beers. You can drink St Austell's beer at *The Star Hotel*, or six miles east of the city on the road to St Austell, *The Hawkin's Arms* at Probus has the same beer in good condition. At Perranarworthal four miles south of Truro, where the main road crosses the river, *The Norway Inn* is an old coaching house, a very attractive building, where you can drink Devenish's ales.

Falmouth, though with much recent building, is still a fascinating town, with the atmosphere of a busy sea-port. Pendennis Castle (16th century), on the promontory with magnificent views, should be visited. Thereafter you can relax with a pint of St Austell in *The Mason's Arms*. Devenish pubs abound all over the town, but one to try is *The Grapes* in Church Street, Devenish's earliest pub in Cornwall, it has a good view of the harbour and is right in the middle of the shopping area.

From Falmouth try the B3291 to the south; as you travel, the scenery gets lusher and greener, with many rhododendrons and fuschias. *The Gweek Inn* is a friendly little place at **Gweek**, at the head of the Helford Estuary; it serves Devenish beer. The road along the estuary to Helford runs through the most charming part of Cornwall. **Helford** is a tiny village on the bank of the river, with abundant flowers and palms. Rows of tiny cottages, stone-walled and thatched, face the creek. There is a foot-ferry across the estuary, half a mile wide here. It is a noted sailing spot, and *The Shipwright's Arms*, an old thatched pub with a terraced garden, is where the yachting fraternity go to drink Devenish's beers, or something stronger.

Helston has more to offer than the annual 'Furry Dance'. It is an ancient town, a borough since 1200, and has some fine houses and streets. Coinagehall Street, which did indeed have a coinage hall, as Helston was one of the towns allowed to mint coins by Edward I, has a stream running down a conduit on each side. This street, too, is important to beer enthusiasts, for *The Blue Anchor Inn* is one of the very few home-brew houses in the country. Behind the little thatched pub, the landlord has his own brew-house, in which he produces his own excellent draught bitter, called Spingo, and, in the winter, he adds a special strong brew. For the sake of comparison, you can drink St Austell beer in town at *The Rodney*.

To the west along the A394 road to Penzance, at the village of **Breage**, where the 15th-century church of St Breaca has fine medieval wall paintings, Devenish's beer is to be had in *The Queen's Arms*. **Penzance** is, of course, well provided with pubs, among which Devenish's *Crown Inn*, Victoria Square, Bread Street, is worth a visit. St Austell's beers are served in

The Yacht Inn. And in the tiny village of **Mousehole**, with its narrow harbour between steep cliffs, Mrs Busby pulls pints of St Austell beer in *The Ship Inn*.

St Ives in its fine situation on St Ives Bay is possibly too well known as a holiday resort and centre for artists, so that it attracts more visitors than can be comfortably assimilated in the summer season. Nevertheless, it is an old borough with many quaint narrow streets and pretty cottages. For local beer, look for *The Castle Inn*, Fore Street, a Devenish house, or *The Lifeboat Inn*, which has St Austell's ales.

WK

Wales and the Borders

Hereford and Worcester, Shropshire, Wales

Shropshire and Hereford are two of the least-known and most agricultural of England's counties. Though so close to the Black Country, they have retained their peace and relative emptiness, even after the arrival of the north–south M5 motorway. Through the change in local boundaries in 1974, Herefordshire rather reluctantly joined Worcestershire, a county with an air which seems more attuned to urban life, with its proximity to Birmingham and manufacturing towns like Kidderminster. But now Hereford and Worcester are one county administratively, different as their traditions and, in many ways, their people are.

One common factor between the new county's two parts is the importance of fruit growing, particularly of apples, pears and hops. Hereford has long been famous for its cider and perry. However, despite the many acres of hop-fields, the county is not particularly brewing country. Hereford's own brewery closed many years ago, and nowadays the most local of Hereford and Worcester's beers come from Burton-upon-Trent, Birmingham and Wolverhampton. There is at least a fair variety to be found.

The two brewers' names most commonly seen are those of subsidiaries of national companies, the giants Bass-Charrington and Allied Breweries (Ind Coope), makers of Double Diamond and Skol Lager.

Mitchells and Butlers (M & B) of Birmingham are part of the Bass-Charrington group, and most of their pubs sell Keg Worthington E, but M and B's pale mild and their bitter are still often available on draught, served by handpump. The bitter, in particular, can be a very palatable drink if well kept, with a more traditional 'hoppy' flavour than their premium bitter, Brew XI, which has a sweetish taste.

Ansells, also of Birmingham, are part of Allied Breweries, and, though they are still brewing their own mild and bitter, the promotion of the group's more expensive national keg beers is tending to take preference. Where you can find Ansells served without CO_2 pressure, it is to be recommended, but you need to look hard for it.

DAVENPORT'S is yet another Birmingham brewer, but remains an independent company, with pubs well scattered over a number of counties. Their draught bitter has been a frequent prize-winner, and they also make a pleasing mild ale. Mild is a much more popular drink in the Midlands and west than it is in the south of England, where often today pubs do not stock it at all. Davenport's draught beers are usually served by electric pump, which often takes the form of a glass container on the bar top, holding a metered half-pint. This system produces an excellent non-gassy glass of beer. They brew a keg bitter and mild (Drum Bitter and Drum Mild) and a range of bottled beers, including a tasty strong ale, Top Brew.

Marston's, the one remaining independent brewery company in Burton-upon-Trent, has a number of pubs in the border counties. Their ordinary bitter is a good sound drink, often served without CO_2 pressure, while their best, Pedigree Bitter, is a very flavoursome ale and quite strong.

Some pubs in the border counties still have a Bass-Worthington sign. They used to belong to the company before it became part of the present Bass-Charrington group, and such pubs often have draught Bass (or Worthington) in the traditional form, not under pressure. It is a superior beer, in my own opinion, to any of the other beers brewed by the group.

Probably the most distinctive beers, those with most claim to be the local beer of Hereford and Worcester, are those of BANKS and HANSON.

The WOLVERHAMPTON AND DUDLEY BREWERIES are one company brewing under two names. Banks' beers come from Wolverhampton, and Hanson's from Dudley, but they are very similar in character, and the pubs use similar signs, a white lion on black or dark brown with either the name Banks' or Hanson's in yellow. They brew draught bitter and mild under both names, but the bottled beer is nearly all Banks'. Mainly served by electric pump, it is as consistently good beer as you are likely to find in the region.

A short way from the Birmingham conurbation is **Kidderminster**, a busy town on the River Stour. You can try Banks' beer at *The Land Oak* (a 'Pint 'n' Platter' house) in

Birmingham Road. On the whole, it is best to avoid the centre of town and look for the Banks' beer in *The Old Bear* in Stourbridge Road, **Broadwaters**, on the A451 on the northern side of town.

In this village *The Hare and Hounds* serves the rare BATHAM'S beer. This is brewed near by at Brierley Hill, but this small family firm has only very few pubs, mainly small locals in out-of-the-way spots.

There is another Batham pub, *The Plough*, in **Shenstone**, to the south-east of Kidderminster on the A450, and also at **Chaddesley Corbett**, some three miles east on the A448 to Bromsgrove, called *The Swan*. Hanson's have *The Talbot* in the same village.

Quite close to Kidderminster on the other side of the Severn is the lovely unspoiled area of the Wyre Forest. The only main road through it is the B4194 from Bewdley. *The Buttonoak* is a fine country pub with a garden in the middle of the Forest, some four miles out of Bewdley; the Banks' beer is very well kept. In **Bewdley**, a town well deserving of exploration, you can drink Davenport's beer at *The Talbot*.

South of here lies one of Worcester's most unusual towns, **Droitwich Spa**, an old Roman spa, whose waters are no longer in demand, but which remains a peaceful town, though close to the M5 motorway. It is well endowed with hotels, including the 16th-century *Raven*. Among the pleasant streets of mellow old red-brick houses is *The Star and Garter*, a friendly Davenport pub, two minutes from the main street.

Just three miles north, across the motorway, is a pleasant Banks' pub, *The Crown* at **Wychbold**, while north along the A442 towards Kidderminster you will find Marston's *New Inn* at **Cutnall Green**, a welcoming little inn with trout fishing.

The city of **Worcester** has, sadly, allowed the traffic to take control, and meandering one-way systems seem to make the roads more crowded, not less so. Some of the houses just to the east of the river seem to be neglected, no doubt due for demolition, though many look worthy of restoration. But there is always the magnificent cathedral overlooking the Severn with, opposite, the County Cricket Ground, which must rival Canterbury in beauty at the height of summer. Worcester is fortunate in having a variety of beers, with *The Cardinal's Hat* in Friar Street serving Davenport's, *The Star*

Hotel in Foregate Street (AA two-star) having Banks' and Mitchells and Butler's draught beers on beer engine in *The Eagle Vaults* in Friar Street. Another more friendly place to find Banks' beer is *The King's Head* in Sidbury, near the cathedral (rooms and snacks available), while Marston's beer can be drunk in *The Red Lion* also in Sidbury.

South of the city lies the Vale of Evesham, with the River Avon flowing through orchards and some delightful villages. Neither Pershore, an attractive little town on the Avon, nor Evesham, which has many fine old houses, offer a selection of local beer, but it is not far to go to one really tranquil and lovely village. Coming out of Pershore along the A44 towards Evesham and London, just over the bridge you will see a lane curving away to the right signposted **Elmley Castle**. About three miles along here you enter a village of mixed 18th-century red-brick and older half-timbered cottages. If you go straight on into the village you come to an apparent dead end in a wide street. On the right is the *Queen Elizabeth*, a most attractive old inn which serves Marston's Burton Beer (not, when last visited, the Draught Pedigree, but well-kept ordinary bitter). This is a good spot to start on a walk to nearby Bredon Hill.

Away across the Avon and Severn valleys lies another hill, or range of hills, The Malverns. At **Great Malvern** Marston's have a comfortable little hotel, *The Red Lion*, well placed for a walking holiday.

North of here on the A44 Worcester–Leominster road you can drink Marston's beer in *The Royal Oak* at **Broadway-on-Teme**, and Banks' beers are to be found at *The Mason's Arms*, **Castle Hill**, about one and a half miles east of Martley on the B4204 road towards Tenbury. Banks' have a delightful, historic residential hotel, too, in **Tenbury Wells**, *The Royal Oak*, Market Street. Crowded with visitors on summer week-ends, it offers excellent meals and snacks and good beer.

Turning southwards along an attractive road, B4124, for nine miles, you come to the quiet, historic market town of **Bromyard**. Among a number of fine old buildings in the High Street is an unspoiled pub, *The Bay Horse*, which has M & B draught Brew XI and mild.

In The Square *The Hop Pole* is a most attractive old country town hotel. Clean and inviting, it is an ideal place for a snack lunch with a pint of Marston's fine Pedigree Bitter. The restaurant is well worth a special visit for dinner.

Farther south through really peaceful countryside is another old market town with many splendid black-and-white buildings. **Ledbury** has a particularly fine early 17th-century half-timbered Market House in the centre of town. *The Feathers* is a very old hotel, serving Whitbread's beers from Cheltenham (on pressure). It is worth seeking out *The Olde Talbot*, New Street, an especially well-kept, friendly pub with rooms and a restaurant; it serves Ansell's bitter by handpump.

Hereford, a city with a beautiful small cathedral and a number of old buildings, is a disappointment for the beer drinker. Most pubs are Whitbread houses—successor to the Cheltenham and Hereford Brewery—and serve Whitbread Trophy or PA, which is brewed in Cheltenham. One has to go to the edge of town to find a pub which has Banks' beer, to *The Cock of Tupsley*, a large modern pub (named after a horse, as the sign shows!) on the Ledbury road. Marston's beer can be drunk at *The Bells* in **Almeley**, a village with some old houses but rather a lot of new bungalows, tucked away off the main Hereford–Kington road, three miles north of Eardisley. It is a small, low pub, and the simple bar parlour has a little open fireplace and old dark wood settles. Marston's Burton bitter and mild are on pressure, but not over-gassed.

The Leominster–Kington A44 road runs through a number of lovely villages of old black-and-white buildings, many of them dating from medieval times. **Eardisland** is distinguished by the little River Arrow, which flows under the main street. Not far from the bridge is *The White Swan*, a small inn, unspoiled and friendly, which serves snacks and Marston's beer.

Kington, only three miles from the Welsh border on the A44, remains a local farmers' town. The pubs and hotels are friendly and have not changed their image to appeal to tourists—and they are the more enjoyable for it.

The Royal Oak, in the main street up the hill towards the church, is a low rustic building, announcing itself as 'the last pub in England'. The main bar is noisy and cheerful, and there is a pretty little garden at the back with views of the hills. Marston's beer is on handpump, and snacks and rooms are available. *The Burton Arms*, just off the main street, is a comfortable AA hotel, with a restaurant. It serves Ansell's draught bitter and mild by handpump in the 'Gentlemen's Bar' and the slightly plusher lounge bar.

Though there is so little regional beer in the area, several pubs have the 'traditional draught' versions of national brews. At **Titley,** four miles out of Kington on the Presteigne road, *The Stag Inn* is a clean pub with well-kept Mitchells & Butler's bitter; you can't miss the enormous 'primitive' painted sign on the wall outside. And at **Lyonshall,** a tiny village on the A480 Hereford road, just past the A44 turn-off three miles east of Kington, *The Royal George,* one of the pleasantest of many Whitbread pubs around, has the Cheltenham-brewed PA on beer engine. This is more of a light bitter, certainly with a cleaner, more bitter taste than M & B's Brew XI.

Also on the Welsh border, and on the bank of the River Wye, **Hay on Wye** is a town of steep, narrow streets and is perfectly situated for walking or pony-trekking in the nearby Black Mountains. Again there is no real local beer, but *The Three Tuns*, a tiny old pub with low ceilings on the corner by the turn to the bridge in Broad Street, has Mitchells & Butler's draught bitter. You have to ask for it though, as it is drawn straight from the cask, and the bar is crammed with various keg beer mountings.

Much farther down the Wye, **Ross on Wye** is a town of many hotels, as it is a centre for the attractive holiday area of the Wye Valley and Forest of Dean. Most of the town stands on a hill high above the river. Near the old market house in the centre you can find proper draught Bass in a friendly little free house, *King Charles II*. It has an attractive frontage, with hanging flower baskets. The bar was being redecorated when last visited, but it looks likely to remain comfortable without being plush. There is also M & B Brew XI on handpump; a drink of this after the Bass makes an interesting comparison. Also in Ross, near the top of steps down to the Wye on the road out towards Hereford, is the *Man of Ross Inn*. A really warm, cosy pub, it has Whitbread's PA served by handpump and the Trophy bitter under pressure.

Shropshire (or Salop, its alternative name), besides being one of England's largest counties, is one of the least spoiled, being comparatively little explored by outsiders. It offers the contrast of wild hill country along the Welsh border or on Long Mynd, with quiet agricultural scenery along the River Severn and the Shropshire Union Canal and the charm of lovely old towns like Ludlow and Shrewsbury.

Brewing is not one of the county's important activities, but there is a fairly wide selection of individual beers, though well scattered. Apart from the national beers, represented most frequently by Mitchells and Butler's and Ansell's (Birmingham offshoots of Bass-Charrington and Allied Breweries respectively), the most easily located local beer is that brewed at **Wem** by GREENALL WHITLEY. Greenall Whitley, which claims to be the largest independent brewery in Britain, brews mainly in Lancashire, at Warrington and St Helen's, but the Shropshire supplies are locally produced.

Greenall Whitley do a draught Best Bitter and a Pale Ale, as well as a more traditional dark mild. They also have their own draught lager, Grunhalle, which is good of its kind, a keg bitter and a good range of bottled beers. Most of their houses serve the draught beer by electric pump, a method more common here than in the south.

Beers from neighbouring Staffordshire include MARSTON's of Burton-upon-Trent, whose pubs tend to be simple and unassuming and whose beer is often very good indeed, and BANKS' from Wolverhampton. From Lancashire you find BURTONWOOD beer, brewed near Warrington, who have a number of pubs in the north of the county and on the Welsh border. BORDER BREWERIES of Wrexham show their red-dragon sign in many places, especially around Oswestry.

More remarkable is that there are two places in Shropshire where you can drink beer made on the premises by the licensee. This is a reminder of the days before the growth of the commercial brewing companies, when it was normal for the publican to brew his own beer. There are very few such pubs left, though two places have begun to brew their own beer in recent years, one in Scotland and a restaurant in Somerset.

At the *All Nations Inn* in Coalport Road, **Madeley** (now part of Telford New Town), about ten miles east of Shrewsbury, Mrs Lewis brews her own pale mild draught ale. The pub is plain and simple, but customers are drawn from quite a distance to try the home-brew. It is appropriate that this traditional approach to brewing should be found so close to the great cradle of industry, the Ironbridge Gorge. Here the Industrial Revolution began, with the first smelting of iron from coke, the world's first iron bridge (at Ironbridge), and here developed Britain's earliest industry. Now many relics of this era are gathered together into a new open-air museum, Ironbridge Gorge Museum.

From Ironbridge itself, a small road runs along the north side of the River Severn towards Coalport. About a mile along is the hill on which was built an inclined plane to bring coal down in tubs from the canal above to the river below. Now it is a quiet little spot, where the Museum Trust is reconstructing as much of the inclined plane as possible *in situ*. On the opposite bank of the river, spanned here by a footbridge, is a little pub, *The Boat*, at **Jackfield**, which serves Banks' excellent Wolverhampton beer. You can get there by road, along the B4376 from Much Wenlock, via Broseley. Still in the Ironbridge area, at **Coalbrookdale** just to the north-west of the Ironbridge, you can try Greenall Whitley's Shropshire beers at *The Valley Hotel*, a residential inn which does snacks and full meals. This is well placed to visit historic Buildwas Abbey, only three miles farther west along the river.

While in this area, you could take the road up Coalbrookdale to Wellington (A4169). This is all now officially designated Telford and is all fairly built up, but as you meet the east–west A5 road you are in Wellington. Turning right here, then taking the left fork towards Newport, you come to **Hadley** in one mile, where you can drink Marston's Burton bitter at *The Summer House*. Another Marston's pub near by, *The Malt Shovel*, has the excellent draught Pedigree Bitter. It is nearly a mile down a minor road to the north at **Lee-gomery** and is very close to the Shropshire Union Canal.

Shrewsbury, some ten miles west, is one of the finest Tudor towns in the country. Almost every street has its quota of magnificent half-timbered houses. The town is in a glorious situation, too, almost surrounded by the Severn and within reach of historical remains, such as the Roman town of Uriconium (Wroxeter today). Alas, most of the finest old taverns in Shrewsbury offer only the ubiquitous national brews, though you could do worse than look into *The Three Fishes Inn* in Fish Street, which has Whitbread's beer.

In Mardol *The Britannia* is a friendly Greenall Whitley hotel facing the river, with bar snacks and meals, while the same beer can be had in *The Unicorn* in Wyle Cop. *The Peacock*, a pub with an unusual series of old arches, has Border beers from Wrexham. It is in Wenlock Road, otherwise you have to leave the middle of town to find distinctive beers. Over the English Bridge, past the Abbey Church, in Sutton Road, is Banks' *The Charles Darwin*, one of their 'Pint and Platter' houses.

On the A49 south out of Shrewsbury running between Long Mynd and Wenlock Edge, Banks' beer can be found at *The Beeches* at **Bayston Hill** (three miles from Shrewsbury). On this road, too, farther south, is the Victorian resort of **Church Stretton**, nestling below Long Mynd and in a splendid situation for walking on these hills. Here Greenall Whitley's beer can be drunk at *The King's Arms* in the High Street.

The main road keeps the railway line company along the valley, and, some eight miles south of Ludlow, both arrive at **Craven Arms**, which is both a cross-roads and a rail junction, where the Mid-Wales line curves off westwards on its rural journey towards Swansea.

The Stokesay Castle in School Road has Davenport's beers and would make a pleasant, if simple place to stay. Its name comes from the actual Stokesay Castle near by, a medieval fortified manor house, which can be visited.

South along the A49 lies **Ludlow**, a satisfying town of old buildings of all ages from Tudor to Georgian. A peaceful town, it has a magnificent castle, towering above the River Teme, where a hired punt provides an hour or more's real relaxation. Architecturally, undoubtedly the finest inn of the town is the famous *Feathers Hotel*, described as 'one of the most elaborate timber and plaster buildings in England' by Maxwell Fraser in *Welsh Border Country*. You will, however, find there only Whitbread's beers. But *The Rose and Crown Hotel*, another interesting building, in Church Street, is a Greenall Whitley house. It has been licensed since the 16th century. Another old-fashioned and interesting Greenall Whitley pub is the oddly named *Keysell's Counting House* in King Street.

Towards Kidderminster the road skirts the southern edge of Clee Hill, and runs into the little village of **Hopton Wafers**. Here *The Crown* is worthy of a visit for its excellent Davenport beers (from Birmingham). Hot and cold bar snacks are to be had with your draught bitter or mild, which are served by handpump. They also have Drum Bitter, if you happen to prefer keg.

If you like Banks' beer, then another three miles farther east at **Cleobury Mortimer**, near the Wyre Forest, you will find it in *The Old Lion*.

On the other side of Ludlow, near the Welsh border, lies the small hilltop town of **Bishop's Castle**. Just to the west off the main A488 Clun–Shrewsbury road, it is very quiet and simple, with steep, narrow streets. Near the top of the town you will see *The Five Tuns*, an attractive, well-kept old building which proudly announces 'Home-brewed beer'. This is the other of Shropshire's two such rare pubs. It is comfortable, gleaming and friendly, and Mr Roberts' own draught bitter and mild are good individual beers.

In Bishop's Castle you can compare Mr Roberts' brew with that of Greenall Whitley by going along to *The Black Lion*, not far away in Welsh Street.

North of here there is a pleasant alternative road to Shrewsbury through Church Stoke, Chirbury and Worthen (B4386). At **Marton** you will find Burtonwood beers from Lancashire at *The Sun Inn*, an attractive residential house with fishing rights on nearby Marton Pool.

Ellesmere is a pleasant market town in the Shropshire 'Lake District'. Here you may want to investigate the interior of a building with an attractive Victorian front. It's the *Black Lion*, where they serve local Border beers from Wrexham. At the back there are some remains of an earlier period, as the house is originally very old. You can drink Border beer too in another old pub, *The White Hart*.

East of here, at **Whitchurch**, a quiet town with some Georgian houses, you can find Burtonwood beer at *The Victoria Hotel*. It is a simple but well-proportioned late-18th-century residential hotel (AA two star).

Market Drayton is a town of more character, just on the eastern edge of the county, with the little River Tern running through it. Here you can find Banks' beer at *The Stormy Petrel*, Tern Hill, and Marston's beers in *The King's Arms*, a pub which provides meals and has fishing available.

Near Market Drayton, Marston's pubs occur in a number of the small villages. At **Hinstock**, on the A41 about six miles south, is the *Four Crosses*, while at **Cheswardine**, three miles east along minor roads, you will come across *The Red Lion*.

Midway between Cheswardine and the even tinier **Goldstone**, it is possible to drink Thwaites' Blackburn beer at *The Wharf Tavern*. The pub is right on the Shropshire Union Canal, by bridge 55, if you are a canal enthusiast. There are good hot and cold snacks. This is the only Thwaites pub in the area.

Oswestry has the air of a border town, with Welsh voices and English rural accents both to be heard, especially on market day. From the Castle Bank, all that remains of the old marcher castle, there is a fine view of the Welsh hills. Oswestry is a good place for seekers after local beer, since Border beers are easily found in the town. Try it in *The Cross Keys*, Cross Street, which was the leading coaching inn when the town was on the London–Holyhead mail route, or in *The Fox Inn*, a medieval half-timbered pub in Church Street. Banks' beer is also available in the town, at *The Unicorn*, near the town centre on Albion Hill. You can also drink Greenall Whitley's Shropshire ales in *The White Lion*.

At nearby **Whittington** (three miles east), a village with a moated castle, the Border 'dragon' can be seen outside *The Penrhos Arms*, a very old house, but quite plain and simple. Also in the village Robinson's Cheshire ales from Stockport are served at *Ye Olde Boote*, a residential house, which overlooks the moat and castle. Robinson's have a number of pubs and hotels throughout North Wales, and their draught bitter is a good, fairly distinctive ale, though sometimes served under pressure.

Oswestry is as good a point as any to enter North Wales, for it is not many miles south of **Wrexham**, a busy border industrial town. Here is situated North Wales' only independent brewery, BORDER BREWERIES LTD.

Seventy years ago there were nineteen breweries in Wrexham alone, and it was in Wrexham around that period that continental-style lager is said to have been first brewed in Britain. Today Allied Breweries still brew their Skol lager in the town.

Border Breweries stem from two older breweries in Wrexham and a third in Oswestry. F. W. Soames and Co. developed in the 19th century from a 'home-brew' public house, *The Nag's Head* (which still stands beside the present brewery), which had been brewing since the 18th century. Elsewhere in Wrexham the Island Green Brewery developed separately until, in 1931, the two companies were merged. A year later they absorbed Dorsett Owen's Brewery in Oswestry and the new name of Border Breweries was established.

Border brew mainly draught mild and draught bitter, but they also have a keg bitter (Dragon Keg) and brew a strong barley wine, Royal Wrexham. Most of their pubs have the beer in casks, which are dry-hopped and fined before being sent out, but some of the draught beer is filtered and chilled in the brewery and sent out as 'tank beer' under CO_2 pressure.

In **Wrexham**, apart from visiting the historic timber-fronted *Nag's Head* by the brewery, you can drink Border ales in *The Old Swan*, an old pub, where the Court Leet of Wrexham Abbot and of Stansty used to be held. *The Horns*, by the bridge over the Gwenfro, is a house which dates from 1702.

Apart from Border ales, there is often a choice of regional beers in North Wales. Signs to look for are the unicorn of Robinson's of Stockport, Greenall Whitley, who supply their Welsh pubs with their Warrington (Lancashire) brew rather than that produced at Wem, Marston's of Burton and, my personal favourite, Burtonwood's, also from Warrington. However, in any house with these signs, whatever their style, you should find beer with a good distinctive taste, though, naturally, the draught beer will vary from place to place, depending on how it is kept.

In the area around Wrexham, Border beers are to be found in *The Cross Foxes* at **Overton Bridge**, six miles south of Wrexham on the A528, where it crosses the River Dee. This is an old inn modernised, a good place for lunch. At **Chirk**, just on the border about seven miles north of Oswestry, *The Hand* serves a good pint of Border bitter and it is an attractive Georgian building. Just a mile along the road, Banks' beer is available in *The New Inn*, **Gledrid**.

Chirk is at the head of the lovely Vale of Llangollen, and the town of **Llangollen**, justly famous for the annual Eisteddfod, is most beautifully sited in its wooded valley. If you want to stay here at a place where you can drink a good pint you might try *The Grapes Hotel*, a comfortable Burtonwood house. Border beer is to be found in *The Smithfield* and Robinson's in *The Bridge End Hotel*, another comfortable place to stay, right beside the fascinating Llangollen canal.

North, between here and the coast, is pretty hill country with some attractive towns, often neglected by visitors on their way to the coastal resorts or Snowdonia. **Ruthin**, on the other side of Llantysilio Mountain from Llangollen, has many old buildings, one of them a delightful, historic inn, *The Wynnstay Arms*. Dating from the mid-16th century, the inn offers rooms and meals as well as Burtonwood's beers. In the middle of town, Robinson's ales can be drunk in *The Wine Vaults*, also an old building, with a colonnade of pillars.

Some eight miles east of Ruthin is the town of **Mold**, in

whose High Street you will find Burtonwood's *Black Lion Hotel*, a pleasant Georgian house. Border beers are served in *The Cross Keys*, a smaller pub with an attractive weatherboarded front. For a most welcoming country inn near here with well-kept beer, take the A494 back towards Ruthin and turn off south after about five miles along B5430 to **Llanarmon**. Here you can enjoy Burtonwood beer served without CO_2 pressure at *The Raven*.

Near the coast and the popular seaside town of Rhyl is the little cathedral city of **St Asaph**, whose cathedral is the smallest of ancient foundations in Britain. *The Kinmel Arms* here has Greenall Whitley's beer. An especially delightful place to drink this beer is at *The Salusbury Arms* at **Tremeirchion**. The village is on a minor road, two miles south of the main A55, three miles east of St Asaph. The inn is in a lovely position on the side of a hill, with a superb view westwards across the Vale of Clwyd. It is an attractive house, and serves evening meals.

On the other side of the valley rise the hills of Denbigh, where charming villages are tucked away in narrow valleys, and where there are some equally charming inns. *The Black Lion* at **Llanfair Talhaiarn** is in a quiet spot beside the old bridge over the River Elwy. This is one of Robinson's Unicorn hotels and well worth a visit.

You can drop down easily from here to the coast at **Abergele** (Marston's beer is in *The Cambrian Hotel*), Colwyn Bay or **Llandudno**, probably the most interesting of the seaside towns, with its two beaches, one on either side of the peninsula and the striking 900-foot Great Orme. Here *The Alexandra* is a Burtonwood house and Greenall Whitley's beer is to be found in *The Albert*. West along the coast road, through Conway, with its ancient castle, you come to **Penmaenmawr**, where you can drink Marston's beers at *The Fairy Glen Hotel*.

Facing the Isle of Anglesey is **Bangor**, a university town and resort. You can stay here at *The Castle Hotel*, where Burtonwood's ales are served, or you can drink Greenall Whitley's beer at *The Antelope*.

Just to the south is the justly famous little town of **Caernarfon**, whose magnificent castle is open to the public and should not be missed. There is no shortage of regional beer here. Try Marston's Burton bitter in *The Anglesey Arms*, a residential hotel beneath the castle, Burtonwood Ales in *The Ship and*

Castle, Bangor Street, or you can have Greenall Whitley's beer in *The Albert*.

Across in Anglesey, the historic town of **Beaumaris** overlooks the Menai Strait and affords a fine view of Snowdon. Burtonwood's ales are worth drinking at *The White Lion*, a pleasantly comfortable hotel. A much older pub in the town is *The George and Dragon*, which was built in 1595, and is full of character. It is possible to stay here, so that you can dispose of several pints of Robinson's beer without having to walk home. Elsewhere on the island, Robinson's sign can be found in **Menai Bridge**, where *The Four Crosses* serves a reliable meal near to the famous suspension bridge. At **Moelfre** on the north coast, where there is a noted lifeboat station, Robinson's have *The Kinmel Arms*, a pub with, as you would expect, a lot of nautical atmosphere. The snacks are reputed to be good too.

At **Pentraeth**, a few miles to the south, it is worth stopping at *The Panton Arms*, an historic building, one of the many inns patronised by George Borrow during his tour of 'Wild Wales'. The beer here is Burtonwood and the hotel has a wide dinner menu. The same beer is to be found in **Holyhead**. If you have time to spare before catching the boat look into *The Albert Vaults* in Market Street. Also in the town *The Prince of Wales* is a large pub which serves Greenall Whitley's beers.

Back on the mainland, we are in Snowdonia, and, if you are looking for a place to stop for a drink or meal near to Snowdon itself, then you should be suited by *The Vaynol Arms* at **Nant Peris** on the main road just south of Llanberis and close to the lake of Llyn Padarn. It has Robinson's beer served by electric pump and rooms to let as well. A short climb from here brings you to the Snowdon Mountain Railway.

West of here, across the hills, the A487 road runs south from Caernarfon to Porthmadog. About eight miles along at Penygroes, a turn east down a B road brings you to **Talysarn**, where in a most welcoming hotel (six bedrooms), ideally placed for fishing or walking, you can drink excellent Marston's Burton beer. It is *The Nantle Vale Hotel*.

In the Lleyn Peninsula, Pwllheli is probably the best-known town because of its holiday camp, and it is a bustling resort in the season, but just four miles farther west is a charming, quiet little seaside village, **Llanbedrog**. Here *The Ship Inn*, a welcoming, residential pub, offers Burtonwood's beer.

Round Tremadog Bay in what was until 1974 the county of Merioneth, but is now part of Gwynedd, **Harlech** with its dominating castle is a town not to be missed. You can find Greenall Whitley beer here in *The Queens*, but about three miles farther south at **Llanbedr** is an especially attractive inn: the 450-year-old *Victoria Hotel*, with its own garden, stands beside the river. The Robinson's beer is worthy of the spot.

Dolgellau is a fine centre for the sea, fishing and walking or climbing. A little stone-built town, it stands near the Mawddach Estuary, not far from the resort of Barmouth. *The Stag* is the place to go for Burtonwood beer. From here across the hills runs a lovely road to **Bala** at the northern end of the lake of the same name. Here we are back in Border Brewery's territory, and *The Goat* (a residential inn) keeps the draught bitter and mild very well. There is Greenall Whitley's Warrington beer too, in the three-star hotel *White Lion Royal*.

If instead of taking the hill road from Dolgellau you choose the southward road you come to **Machynlleth**, a little market town in the Dovey Valley at the meeting point of the coastal road and the east–west road from Shrewsbury and Welshpool. Here is one of the fairly rare places in Wales in which to drink Banks' Wolverhampton beer, in *The White Lion*, a comfortable two-star hotel in the middle of town. The traditional draught beer is served by electric pump, Banks' usual way of dispensing it. There is another Banks' house not far away at **Talybont**, some ten miles south along the A487. It is also called *The White Lion* and serves snacks.

Following the Dovey Valley from Machynlleth, the main A458 turns east at Mallwyd between the peaks of Tir Rhiwiog (1787 feet) and Garnedd Wen (1716 feet) and runs through lovely hill country to **Welshpool** on the River Severn. Near by is Powys Castle (13th century and open to the public) and the Welshpool and Llanfair narrow-gauge railway. Burtonwood beers can be found at *The Crown Inn*.

We are back near the English border here, and the Border Brewery's red dragon sign can be seen, in particular at **Bwlch y Cibau** on the A490, eight miles north of Welshpool, where *The Cross Keys* is a modernised pub with some attractive ornamental ironwork. *The Horseshoes* at **Llanyblodwel**, a tiny village off the A495 about eight miles south of Oswestry, is the oldest of Border's pubs. It is a lovely half-timbered building.

South of Welshpool, and still close to the border and the Severn, stands the little town of **Montgomery**, formerly the county town, before the county was submerged into the new, large Powys. Here look for Burtonwood ales in *The Bricklayer's Arms*. **Newtown**, farther along the Severn, is a little town which has recently been revitalising its light industrial and commercial life and is now busy and thriving. Burtonwood beers are served in *The Pheasant*, a pleasant neo-Tudor pub in the centre of town, or you can drink Border ales in *Castle Vaults*. Worth a detour for its welcome, its Border beers and its setting is *The Red Lion* at **Trefeglwys**. The village is in the hills west of Newtown. You can turn off the main road at Caersws on to the B4569. Here you are not far from the source of the Severn.

By now we are really in mid-Wales, for many the most attractive part of the country, with heather- and gorse-covered hills and quiet villages. It is also the least-populated part of Wales.

There are many free houses in this area, the majority of which serve national keg beers. In this area, too, you will see the signs of Welsh Brewers, together with the red triangle of Bass-Charrington, who control the company. Sometimes an old Hancock's sign is to be seen. Hancocks no longer exists, and Welsh Brewers beer is what you can get in these pubs. There is usually Bass Special on pressure, or Allbright, a light bitter, which has, to my taste, more flavour, and has the advantage of being cheaper also. Bass-Charrington's Welsh Brewers beers are made in Cardiff, and are to be found all over mid and south Wales.

Another common sign is that of Whitbread, who took over the Rhymney brewery near Monmouth. Some Rhymney signs remain, and the Whitbread PA or Trophy bitter in these pubs is usually brewed at Rhymney.

The main road through mid Wales is the A44, formerly the coaching route from Worcester to Aberystwyth. Close to the border the B4594 branches off to the south, and three miles along this winding road you reach **Gladestry**. The village has only a few houses and one shop. *The Royal Oak* is an old, stone-built house, with flagstone floors, huge fireplaces and low ceilings. Since taking it over as a free house, Mr and Mrs Ritchie have added some simple but comfortable bedrooms, so that it is now a marvellous place to stay for a quiet walking holiday close to Offa's Dyke Path. Despite improving the cleanliness and facilities, the Ritchies have not lost the character of a truly local pub, where darts matches and the local game of quoits are played. The beer is Welsh Brewers on pressure.

On the main road to Llandrindod Wells (until the creation of Powys the county town of Radnorshire, reputedly the only county in Britain without traffic lights) there is a very old wayside inn, known to travellers since the old coach road was first used. *The Forest Inn* stands at the turning off towards Builth Wells. A low, rambling, slightly disorganised sort of building, it has fine views of the hills of Radnor Forest. The nearest village is, I suppose, **Llanfihangel Nantmelan**, itself only a couple of houses, just a mile to the east, and two miles from New Radnor. A free house, *The Forest Inn* usually has Mitchells and Butler's draught bitter served by handpump, but it is often out of stock. If you don't like the keg beer (Bass Export) you can always try the draught Taunton vintage cider.

Finding good local beer in mid Wales is a hard task, but in **Builth Wells**, a grey stone town on the Wye, you can find at least one pub which serves Welsh Brewers' draught pale mild without CO_2 pressure. It is *The White Horse* in the High Street.

Brecon, the county town of Powys and an attractive old town on the River Usk, can offer, at any rate, traditional draught Worthington in *The Wellington Hotel*. Fresh Wye salmon is usually on the dining-room menu in season. Not far to the east, along the Brecon–Abergavenny canal, **Crickhowell** crouches below the stern-looking Black Mountains. Here is something of an oasis for the seeker after distinctive beer, for *The Beaufort Arms*, a residential inn, has Davenport's Birmingham beer.

Banks' excellent draught bitter and mild can, surprisingly, be found in the attractive seaside university town of **Aberystwyth**. Here I tracked it down at *Downie's Vaults*, a plain little pub in Eastgate. When the London Philharmonic Orchestra plays in the town, according to landlord Mr Rudge, the players adjourn to this pub after concerts to enjoy the traditional draught beer.

South Wales, perhaps because of its industrial base, has always been notable for its breweries. As in most places, the many independent companies have been gradually whittled away by mergers and take-overs. But still several completely independent local breweries survive.

S. A. BRAIN & Co. of **Cardiff** are the local brewers for the main industrial and mining region around Swansea, Cardiff and Newport. Brewing has been carried on at their present site, The Old Brewery in St Mary Street near the castle, since 1713. Their best-selling traditional draught beers are a dark mild (very popular in South Wales), called Red Dragon (RD), but often known as Brain's Dark, Bitter, and a best bitter called SA, which is somewhat stronger and faintly sweeter. Their draught beers are almost always served by handpump. Brains have a lot of traditional 'local' pubs all over their trading area, but several are of interest, and the beer is almost always good. In **Cardiff,** close to the brewery in St Mary Street, you can drink Brain's Dark in *The Albert,* which does meals and snacks, or, in the same street, try *Cardiff Cottage,* a pleasant small pub. In the northern outskirts of Cardiff, near Llandaff Cathedral, there is *The Black Lion* in Cardiff Road, **Llandaff.**

At the eastern edge of Brain's trading area, where it is hard to find good regional beer, Brain's have *The Blinkin' Owl* in **Cwmbran,** some three miles north of Newport. And at **St Brides Wentloog,** a village just to the south-west of Newport by the mouth of the Usk, the strangely named *Church House* is another Brain's pub.

In Gwent (Monmouthshire) the inn-signs seem to be mainly Whitbread, Welsh Brewers or Ansell's, but if you are near **Abergavenny,** visit *The Station Hotel,* a good plain pub serving Davenport's beers.

In **Porthcawl,** a popular seaside resort, with splendid limpet-covered rocks, *The Pier* is the place to look for local Brain's beers. It is on the Esplanade. Perhaps more peaceful is *The Jolly Sailor* at **Newton,** about two miles out of town along the main road.

Swansea is both industrial and seaside town, a good jumping-off point for the lovely Gower Peninsula. Brain's beer is available at *The Adam and Eve* in the High Street. Here we are also on the edge of another brewer's territory, BUCKLEY'S of Llanelli. In the northern suburb of Llandore you can try their beer in *The Cooper's Arms,* a busy ale house.

Llanelli is a steel- and tin-making town some nine miles west of Swansea on the coast. It is remarkable, too, for the fact that it has two independent breweries. BUCKLEY'S BREWERY LTD. is the larger of the two. It has its brewery in the centre of town, where it was established in the mid-18th century. One of the founders, the Reverend James Buckley, was a Methodist minister, a follower and friend of Charles Wesley, who often stayed with him in Llanelli. The present chairman is a descendant in the direct line of Buckleys.

Buckley's draught beers include SB (Standard Bitter), BB (Best Bitter) and Mild. The individual casks—all metal nowadays, for longer life and greater cleanliness—are fined before being sent out, and often a light covering of CO_2 is put on. They also brew a keg bitter, which is the same as the best bitter, but chilled and filtered. To my taste it is one of the few keg bitters which retains a real beery flavour. The BB is a very clean, bitter drink, and well worth seeking out when in Buckley's trading area.

In Llanelli you should visit *The Stradey Arms* at Furnace on the northern side of town on the Carmarthen road. This village inn has been carefully modernised and now offers good bar meals in a pleasant setting. The beer is on light pressure.

THE FELINFOEL BREWERY is actually at Felinfoel, a northern suburb of Llanelli. It began as a 'home-brew' house in the middle of the 19th century. The present brewery was built in 1878 and continues to brew independently for the eighty or so pubs in the area around. As early as 1935 the brewery began to can beer, following the adoption of beer-canning in the USA about three years before. It was begun to help the local tin-plate industry during depression years. Canned Double Dragon Ale is still one of their most popular lines.

Felinfoel produce a draught bitter, a stronger bitter (Double Dragon) and a mild. As well as Double Dragon they can Double Strong, an especially alcoholic pale ale. Their pubs often have an inscription in Welsh on their signs—'Cwrw Felinfoel' meaning 'Felinfoel Ales'.

North of the town at the village of **Llannon**, on the road to Llandeilo, *The Red Lion* is a pleasant Felinfoel pub, and you can drink this same beer at *Norton Arms* in the village of **Penygroes** about five miles farther north and just off the main road. At **Ammanford** near by, look for Buckley's beer at *The Plough and Harrow*.

Other places to try these local Welsh beers include the comfortable *Ashburnham Hotel* at **Pembrey**, beside Ashburnham Golf Club on Carmarthen Bay five miles west of Llanelli. This is a Buckley's house. North-west of here, Felinfoel's ales are in *The Mason's Arms* at **Kidwelly**, one of very few thatched pubs in this part of Wales.

In the historic town of **Carmarthen** there are several Buckley's and Felinfoel pubs, but you might try Felinfoel ales in *The Drover's Arms*, which has a steak bar at the back in converted stables.

From Carmarthen the main A40 runs towards the coast at Haverfordwest. **St Clears** is a small village at a road junction nine miles from Carmarthen where you can stop for a pint of Felinfoel ale and a grill at Mrs Howell's *Penyrheol Tavern*.

From here the A4066 road leads southwards to the famous Pendine Sands, where in the twenties Sir Malcolm Campbell and John Parry Thomas repeatedly broke each other's world land-speed records. *The Beach Hotel* at **Pendine** was, as the plaque outside reads, the headquarters of all these record attempts by the two great motorists, and the cars were worked on in the hotel garage. You can still drink Buckley's beers at this well-situated hotel, even if you won't see any racing cars these days.

You should find enough evidence to prove that Welsh beer is still going strong—in the commercial as well as alcoholic sense. Unlike the situation in less fortunate Scotland, traditionally-brewed local beer is not too difficult to find in Wales and is usually worth seeking out.

WK

North-west

Cheshire, Lancashire, Cumbria, the Isle of Man

Cheshire makes a fine county to commence our tour of the North-west: a land of good cheese and fine timber-built houses. In beer terms only one brewery is to be found—that of FREDERIC ROBINSON, of Stockport whose story can be traced back to the purchase in 1838 of the Unicorn Inn. In its time Robinson's have absorbed Schofield's Portland brewery, Kay's Atlas brewery of Manchester and Bell's, also of Stockport. Today the fifth generation of Robinsons control the business, which has some 300 houses that display the white unicorn sign against a pale-blue background. Two traditional draught ales are brewed by Robinson's, a Best Mild, which is on the light side, and a Best Bitter, which is well hopped.

A good starting-point is the *Royal Oak* in Stockport Road, **Cheadle**, which serves good bar snacks, and from where you can visit outstanding Bramhall Hall, a fine Elizabethan half-timbered house, set in a magnificent 62-acre park. While in the area you may also like to visit the diminutive *Church Inn*, Ravenoak Road, **Cheadle Hulme**, where Robinson's is available on draught.

A few miles to the south along the A34 is **Alderley Edge**, where you will find a good pint of Robinson's Best Bitter at *The Moss Rose*, which lies off Heyes Lane at the end of an unmade road. The pub boasts a good bowling green and a terrace where you can follow the sport. From here you can go virtually due east to the quiet village of **Prestbury**, where the *Legh Arms* has quite a reputation. The inn dates back to 1423, when it was known as the Saracen's Head. Today it is equally renowned for its food and its Robinson's Best Mild on draught.

Bollington lies across the A523 and makes a good place to stay for a few days. *The Holly Bush* has pleasant rooms, as well as Robinson's beers; you will find the pub at the foot of the hill near the church. The nearby mill town of **Maccles-**

field serves a wide variety of good beers, many of them by handpump. I would particularly single out *The British Flag* in Coare Street, which sells draught Old Tom, a barley wine of distinction, normally only available in bottle form in other Robinson's houses. Alternatively, a Burtonwood pint may be sought at the 17th-century *Old King's Head* in **Gurnett**, which lies by the canal near to where James Brindley, the canal builder, served his apprenticeship.

Take the A536 out of Macclesfield in the direction of Congleton, to find a delightful farm which also doubles as a Robinson's house, *The Harrington Arms* at **Gawsforth**. The bitter is drawn straight from the casks that lie on the floor. A ghost is said to haunt the pub, and yet the whole atmosphere is one of Cheshire tranquillity. Almost due east, in the village of **Sutton**, you can find Robinson's in *The Albion* in London Road and Boddington's beer at *Church House*. Boddington's Bitter is well hopped and a local favourite, although Cheshire pubs sell probably at least as much mild. When you have the time do not miss Little Moreton Hall at **Astbury** near Congleton, a great moated manor house with latticed windows, a still complete Banqueting Hall and a real atmosphere of history—what a spot for a real ale feast! Astbury itself is a hamlet with charming old houses that boast cobbled fore-courts. Here Robinson's have *The Egerton Arms*, with pleasant overnight accommodation, and, near by, *The Horse-shoe* at **Newbold**.

Off the beaten track, only a mile or so from Little Moreton Hall, you will find refreshment in **Smallwood**, which lies to the east of the A50. Here the smart *Legs of Man* serves Robinson's Best Mild. Just within the Cheshire county boundary lies **Church Lawton**, north of Kidsgrove. Here, another Robinson's house, *The Red Bull*, offers both good bitter and bar snacks to the thirsty canal-side walker. Just outside, on the other side of the M6 from Church Lawton, is **Haslington**, where a cosy atmosphere and a good glass of Robinson's on draught await you at the *Hawk Inn*.

Tetley from Leeds and Greenall Whitley from Warrington are the main choices in the railway town of **Crewe**; I would suggest that you try Greenall's *Spread Eagle* in Ludford Street, one of the smallest bars in Cheshire, perhaps in North-west England. North-west of Nantwich at **Tiverton** you will find a very different pint in the form of McEwan's draught at *The Crown* in Four Lane Ends, though I prefer the

Rising Sun in **Tarporley**, a few miles to the north of the A51; this is a Robinson's house, and a good spot to use as your base to visit North Wales. Perhaps good Robinson's draught and pub charm can be seen even better at the *Alveney Arms* in **Cotebrook**, not far from Oulton Park, a noted motor-racing circuit. This Georgian inn has an exquisite cobbled forecourt and a fine porch.

Nearer Wales is the fine town of **Chester**, where Higson's Liverpool-brewed bitter may be enjoyed at the *Bull & Stirrup* in Upper Northgate Street. Holt's beers can be tasted in *The Griffin* in Long Lane. At **Marple** you will find an excellent Robinson's pint at the *Navigation Hotel*, Stockport Road; this pub used to be the brewing house of Sam Oldknow, who built the Peak Forest canal in the 1790s and brewed ale for both the millworkers and navvies. Today you can build up thirst and an appetite by walking along the towpath and seeing no less than seventeen locks.

Romiley, just north-east of Stockport on the A560, houses *The Forester's Arms* in Greave, where many darts matches are played over the BODDINGTON'S ale. There is an old-world charm at the *Forester's* which is apt, as Boddington's can rightly claim to be Manchester's oldest brewery. Boddington's started brewing in 1778 in the Strangeways district of Manchester, to the north-west of Romiley, outside the Manchester boundary, to escape the grain tax which those within the town were compelled to pay to the grinding mills belonging to the grammar school.

Apart from Boddington's draught bitter look for both the dark-coloured and slightly sweet mild and the stronger Best Mild. Increasingly pubs are serving this by metered electric pump.

South of Romiley on the B6103, the sprawling village of **High Lane** is rewarding, for it houses Boddington's *Bull's Head* on the canal bank, with a garden and play area. The village is close to magnificent Lyme Park, with its splendid Georgian mansion of Palladian design, which also incorporates part of an earlier Elizabethan house; it is open from May to October. Beyond **Poynton** on the A523 towards Macclesfield, where you will find Robinson's bitter at *The Farmer's Arms* in Park Lane and the *Bull's Head*, which offers Boddington's, the village of **Adlington** has a canalside pub, *The Miner's Arms*, which also has Boddington's beers.

Lancashire boasts a multitude of brewers. The national Watney has a subsidiary in WILSON's of Manchester, whose sign is a checkerboard; Whitbread brew in **Salford** under the name THRELFALLS (one brew is Chester's Best Mild) and also in **Liverpool** under the same name. DUTTON's, another Whitbread subsidiary, produces a dark mild in **Blackburn**, while TETLEY, an Allied Breweries company, brew in **Warrington** and have some 1150 houses in the Manchester–Liverpool region. Their sign is a rider on horseback. This originates from the former Walker's of Warrington.

Outside Manchester to the south-east on the A57 lies **Denton**, where you have a choice of traditional beer. Boddington's is to be found along the Hyde road at the *Lowes Arms*, while Robinson's on draught can be enjoyed at the *Chapel Inn* in Two Trees Lane, which also has rooms.

Taking the A62 out of Manchester towards the towns and villages where cotton reigned as the staple industry, you will find Robinson's draught at the *Church Inn* in **Failsworth** and, on the main Oldham road, Boddington's at *The Lamb*. I have a preference for the oddly named *Smut Inn* at **Hollinwood** that lies farther on up the same Oldham road; this Boddington's pub takes its name from a farm dog who lived here when the place was a farmhouse in the early Victorian age, and not from any suggestion of smokiness! **Oldham** is *the* town for spinning cotton and can be justly proud of its monumental town hall, which is a copy of Ceres' Temple in Athens. The OLDHAM BREWERY COMPANY brews both a good bitter and slightly sweet, dark-coloured mild at their brewery in Coldhurst Street. Their pubs often announce outside 'An OB House'. Try one of their draught ales at *The Bath* in Union Street.

If you take the A627 Rochdale road out of Oldham, but turn off right to **Shaw**, good snacks and lunches are to be had at the *Blue Bell*, a Robinson's house. **Rochdale** itself is known for Gracie Fields and also as the birthplace of the Co-operative Movement. The town is hilly and has many quaint corners. Many brewers are represented here, including DANIEL THWAITES of Blackburn at *The Brunswick* in Baillie Street and Boddington's at the *Hare & Hounds* in Belfield Road. The B6222 takes you to **Bury**, another industrial town, but well worth visiting on account of the curious pub, *Sir Robert Peel*. This is a new pub opened by Boddington's on the Sunny Bank Road on the Unsworth estate and has fifty-three truncheons displayed in the lounge bar as well as replicas of watchmen's lamps that date back several centuries.

The road westwards from Bury leads to **Bolton** and to a good Boddington's pint at the *Prince William* in Bradshaw-gate, from where you can set out to see two fine half-timbered houses on the northern edge of the town: Smithills Hall and Hall-i'th'-Wood, dating respectively from the 14th and 15th centuries. The latter property saw the composition of Samuel Crompton's important spinning machine, and is therefore a landmark in modern economic history.

If you feel like a break by the side of a canal, turn south to **Worsley**, where Boddington's *Bridgewater Hotel* in Barton Road provides a restful pint and the opportunity to play a pub game. **Salford**, just outside Manchester to the north-west, presents the chance to taste the beer of a different brewer, JOSEPH HOLT of Cheetham, Manchester, in *The Wellington* in Bolton Road. This is a new house, although there are many other Holt's outlets in the immediate vicinity. Holt's brew a dark-coloured draught mild and a traditional Lancashire bitter.

South-west of Salford Boddington's have a recently modernised pub, *The Coach & Horses*, on the Liverpool road in **Cadishead**, which incidentally has some good bar snacks. You are now within a short distance of Warrington-based brewer, GREENALL WHITLEY, whose draught Best Bitter you will no doubt enjoy at *The Plough* in Kenyon Lane in the village of **Croft**; take the B5212 from Cadishead and turn left at Newchurch towards St Helens. Greenall Whitley is one of the independent giants in the brewing world, with breweries at Wem in Shropshire and at St Helens, as well as Warrington. Their sign is a goddess blowing a horn, summoning true ale enthusiasts to their full-bodied mild, their light Pale Ale and their Best Bitter. They also brew Festival Keg. One Greenall bottled beer, Old Chester Ale, is worth trying for its sweet, strong flavour.

In **Warrington** itself you may like to try Greenall's drawn through the traditional handpump at the *Royal Oak* in Bridge Street; alternatively, you can taste another brewer's local ale in **Burtonwood**, on the outskirts of St Helens. Here the *Elm Tree* offers draught bitter from Burtonwood brewery, many of whose pubs use electric pumps. The other Burtonwood draught is a dark mild, popular in the summer months. In **St Helens** you can compare Burtonwood ale at the *Prince of*

Wales in Ormskirk Street with Boddington's at *The Talbot* in Duke Street. The town well warrants a visit on account of the splendid glass museum and the finest modern carillon in Europe.

The road between St Helens and Liverpool takes you through **Prescot**, where the *Hare & Hounds* in Warrington Road presents one of the first opportunities of enjoying HIGSON'S well-flavoured bitter. This Liverpool brewery was founded in the late 18th century and uses the mythical liver bird within an oast house as its mark. Many of its landlords still pull by handpump and sell both bitter and mild in draught form. Note, too, their bottled barley wine, Stingo Gold.

Of the many **Liverpool** pubs to choose from I would select the *Crow's Nest* in Victoria Road, Great Crosby, the *Grapes* in Mathew Street and the *Wheatsheaf* in East Prescot Road, all of which serve Higson's draught.

North of St Helens is the lovely village of **Up Holland**, with its stern stone-built houses that cluster around the 14th-century church. Boddington's *Plough & Harrow* on the Ormskirk Road is an old-world pub in the same tradition. Here a good game of darts can often be had over some of Lancashire's best pub snacks and a good pint. Near Ormskirk the attractively named *Ring O'Bells* in **Lathom** as well as the *Yew Tree* in Grimshaw Lane, **Ormskirk** itself, both offer Higson's. The August flower show in seaside **Southport** gives one the additional opportunity to enjoy Higson's at the *Guest House* in Union Street. (Do not be put off by the name!) East of here on the A565 you will find Higson's, too, at *The Legh Arms*, Mere Brow, **Tarleton**.

Off the M6 the hamlet of **Wrightington** is reached from junction 27 north-west along the B5250. Here the diversion will be well worth while, for draught Burtonwood can be had while enjoying a pub game or two in the *Scarsbrick Arms*, Wood Lane. South of Preston is **Walton-le-Dale**, where Cromwell defeated the Scots in 1648; today the church is well worth a visit, and refreshment may be obtained at Boddington's *White Bull*. In **Preston** try one of the town's oldest houses, the *Old Black Bull* in Friargate, for character. This is a tall, narrow, half-timbered building with a steep gable where I have enjoyed Boddington's on draught and a good lunch. There are rooms also available. In Preston several outlets belong to DANIEL THWAITES, brewers of Blackburn, one of the last still to use shire horses. Their dark mild is brewed particularly to suit the Lancashire taste, while the bitter has perhaps wider appeal. Thwaites also brew a sweeter ale, draught Best Mild. Lovely names are given to their bottled beers, several of which will improve in bottle; these include Old Dan, an extra-strength dark ale, and Big Ben, a dark-coloured strong beer.

The Moorbrook in Preston's North Road is a good starting-point to enjoy Thwaites' ales. If you take the A59 out of Preston another Thwaites house can be found on the Ribchester Road at **Clayton-le-Dale**, which lies between the A59 and A677; this is the *Bonny Inn*, which has a real old-world atmosphere. The pub was once an old weaving mill and later a coach house. If you have a lunch there over a glass of Thwaites' ale ask for a window seat overlooking the countryside and Stonyhurst College in particular.

Blackburn is the home of another Lancashire brewer, MATTHEW BROWN, as well as housing some fine churches. Brown's mark is a red lion; they make two draught beers, although they are increasingly going over to keg and to serving their traditional beers under top pressure. They produce a well-hopped bitter and a dark mild. West of Blackburn you may like to try Brown's at *The Lord Nelson* in **Brindle** on the B5256; this pub was a tannery in the late 17th and early 18th centuries. The mile-iron outside the house (not mile-stone) states 'Walton Summit one miles' in the plural! The original beams, stone fireplaces and half-timbered exterior of nearby *Ye Old Hob Inn* are another good reason to try Brown's beer; it stands only 200 yards from the M6 motorway, exit 29 at **Bamber Bridge**. This pub was once a post-house on the coach route from Edinburgh to London.

If you are travelling south of Darwen you will enjoy the draught ale at *The Red Lion* in **Blacksnape** on the old Roman road from Turton to Darwen. This house serves Burtonwood's and a good range of evening grills in the character of the 17th-century coaching inn it once was. On the north side of Blackburn a welcome pint of Thwaites greets you after walking or driving up the steep B6478 at **Slaidburn**. Here the *Hark to Bounty Inn*, known until the Victorian Age from the 13th century as 'The Dog', serves delightful food—including venison—as well as Thwaites' bitter.

The coastal countryside of St Anne's and Blackpool

beckons. *En route* you will no doubt enjoy a good glass of Boddington's ale at *The Ship Inn* in Bunker Street, **Freckleton**, on the A584 from Preston. The house overlooks the creek of the River Ribble, and the pub has a nautical atmosphere. I always like the good collection of brass as well as the sea charts and local paintings. If you like to get out to the country from the busy seaside resorts I can strongly recommend Boddington's *The Grapes* in the charming village of **Wrea Green**, west of Kirkham. The journey for the draught bitter and charming Lancashire scene with a church reflected in the duck pond of the village green is well worth it.

At the mouth of the Wyre estuary **Fleetwood**, an attractive holiday centre, almost due north of Blackpool, presents the chance to enjoy Boddington's on draught at *The Mount* on the Esplanade and to have a game on their miniature golf course. Inland towards the M6 you will find a Matthew Brown's house, the *Eagle & Child*, in High Street, **Garstang**. This is a small pub but full of character and with genuine traditional ale on draught.

Farther north towards Lancaster takes one towards the outlets of YATES & JACKSON, whose site in Lancaster itself has been a point for brewing since Charles II's reign. Yates & Jackson's draught mild is not nearly as sweet as many others but their bitter is a good Lancashire example of the well-hopped style, often dispensed from wooden casks. **Galgate** on the Preston–Lancaster A6 road makes a good stopping point to try either of these brews, at the *Green Dragon*; while across the estuary the village of **Overton**, south-east of Heysham, has good Yates & Jackson ale at *The Ship*.

Lancaster is worth visiting on account of the University and splendid castle which Elizabeth I enlarged to defend the town against the Spanish Armada. The July regatta presents a good excuse to down a few glasses of the town's other brewer's ales, MITCHELL'S of Moor Lane. Some of their pubs are identifiable by the red rose insignia and the castle trade mark. Mitchell's brews not only a dark mild and a standard bitter but also a higher Original Gravity Bitter, known as Extra Special. They also bottle a stout at the same OG.

Of the many pubs in **Lancaster** I could mention Mitchell's *Tramway* in St Leonard's Gate and their *Ring O'Bells* in King Street, while Yates & Jackson's ales can be bought at *The Sun* in North Road and in *The White Lion* in Bulk Street.

North of the town on the A5105 at **Hest Bank** Boddington's *Hest Bank Hotel* provides tradition by the hotel's 'Beacon Window' where the lantern was placed to guide travellers across the sandbanks. Just beyond neighbouring Carnforth is Leighton Hall, an early neo-Gothic house that is open on Wednesday and Sunday afternoons from May to September.

Warton is a small village to the north where refreshment can be obtained at the *West View*, a Boddington's house that is popular with Americans on account of the memorials in the church to the ancestors of George Washington.

Across Morecambe Bay is the thriving market town of **Ulverston**, known both for the production of fine violins and as the site of HARTLEYS' brewery, which was founded some six years before George III ascended the throne. Hartleys' pubs can be recognised from some distance by the deep-blue sign. *The Old Friend's* in Soutergate and the *Rose & Crown* in King Street both serve good traditional Hartleys' beer.

The Lake District presents a wealth of delightful villages, many of which serve good ale. Hartleys' beer features in several, including the *Outgate Inn* near **Hawkshead** on the B5286 west of Windermere, three-quarters of a mile from Ambleside. The inn has several rooms and the attraction of the nearby ferry service to Bowness. Not far away is the home of Beatrix Potter at Hill Top.

There are no independent breweries in Westmorland, now part of Cumbria, but several neighbouring centres supply good ale. In **Kendal**, famed for its mint cake and castle ruins, a good pint of Yates & Jackson's bitter can be enjoyed at *The Globe Inn* in the Market Place. Although partially rebuilt, it retains some of the old beams. *The Globe*'s one room has been built on a split-level plan with low dividing walls in Cumberland slate. The beer is still served from the wood. A good day to visit the town is on a Saturday when the market is held as it has been since 1189.

Milnthorpe lies south of Kendal on the A6 where Hartleys' *Cross Keys* has a pleasant atmosphere. In contrast, the holiday resort of **Bowness-on-Windermere** lies on the shore of the largest lake in the national park and is the centre of boating activity, particularly in the summer months. Here Hartleys' ales can be enjoyed at the historic *New Hall* in Robinson Place or *The Albert*, both of which at the time of my visit served pints from traditional wooden barrels. The landlords feel strongly that this is a contributory factor to the success of Hartleys' beers, for it allows the fermentation to continue more naturally.

The two Cumberland brewers—JENNINGS and CUMBRIA, formerly known as the Workington Brewery—are at Cockermouth and Workington respectively. Jennings use no top pressure in their delivery systems, but serve ale only by traditional methods in all but two of their houses. In **Cockermouth** itself I would enjoy their well-hopped bitter or dark mild at *The Huntsman* or *The Grey Goat*. If you take the road west to **Great Broughton** you will find the house where Wordsworth was born in 1745; in the village Jennings' good draught beer is found in the *Punch Bowl Inn*. The other direction down the B5292 provides walking opportunities and good ale, also from Cockermouth, at the *Horse Shoe Inn* in **High Lorton**. There are many other delightful villages supplied with Jennings' ale, including **Threlkeld** (*The Horse & Farrier*), the *Drover's Rest* at **Monkhill** and the *Sun Inn* at **Torpenhow.**

Cumbria Brewers at Workington make a bitter under the John Peel XXX brand and call their nutty mild 'Barley Brown' Best. The *Royal Oak* in Pow Street, **Workington**, makes a good first point to try the town's ales, but farther afield you may enjoy them at *The Woolpack* in Main Street, **Keswick**, and at many free houses.

Incidentally, the Government's only nationalised brewery, in Carlisle, was sold off some years ago. Today T & R THEAKSTON'S of Masham near Ripon, Yorkshire, have brought their considerable expertise to the Carlisle brewery and are increasingly brewing for the free trade in Cumbria.

Across the water on the Isle of Man there are two breweries: the CASTLETOWN in Victoria Road, **Castletown**, and OKELL'S in **Douglas.** Lower duty charged by the Manx Government means that the true pint costs that little bit less on the Isle of Man. There are, too, penalties for using synthetic substitutes in the manufacture of beer which the London government might well adopt. Most Castletown pubs are painted black and white and offer two draught ales: a well-balanced bitter and a mild. They also bottle a splendid barley wine that goes under the name of Castletown Liqueur. Okell's sometimes trades under the names of Heron & Brearley and Manington's, but frequently the sign of the falcon is depicted. Okell's, like Castletown, brew two draught ales.

In Castletown itself try the bitter at Okell's *The Glue Pot*, which is down by the harbour, or Castletown's ale in the *Union* in Arbory Street. Outside the main towns *The Foxdale* in **Foxdale**, almost due north of Castletown, makes a good stopping-point for Castletown Mild, but the pub does not open on Sundays during the winter. If you would like both accommodation and a good pint of Okell's, try the *Falcon's Nest* in **Port Erin**, in the south-west corner of the island, from where I have made an interesting trip to Milner Tower at Bradda Head.

CG

Yorkshire and the North-east

The sprawling county of Yorkshire, split now into several parts, boasts no fewer than eight independent brewers, of whom all but the York-based YORKSHIRE CLUBS' BREWERY'S products are likely to be encountered far and wide. In fact, THEAKSTON'S of Masham—pronounced 'Massam' by the locals—have extended their free-trade territory by purchasing the plant of the former State-owned Carlisle brewery.

The University and steel town of **Sheffield** is a good place to start one's journey. Here the few bar pulls of WARD'S still yield good malty flavoured bitter and a higher gravity best. Many enjoy the mild, which can, however, be spoilt on occasion by excessive carbon dioxide. In this event, apart from the gold barley sheaf of Ward's, the Robin Hood symbol of HOME'S occasionally welcomes one, although it is brewed in Nottinghamshire. Try the well-hopped Home's bitter at the delightfully decorated *Pomona*, a small pub on the Eccleshall road in Sheffield.

Through Barnsley it is not far to the wool-making town of **Wakefield** with its fine Georgian houses. I have enjoyed good pints at *The Black Rock* in the Bull Ring, a Tetley house which is a division of Allied. You will see the red-coated huntsman sign through much of the North. By comparison TIMOTHY TAYLOR'S beer can be enjoyed south-east at **Kirkburton** at *The Woodman*. Handpumps are in use in many of the Taylor pubs, serving no less than four draught ales: Landlord, which is a dark mild, Best Bitter, which has good character, Golden Best, Light Mild and Old, a high-gravity dark ale.

Several different brews are to be found at **New Mill**, east of Holmfirth, including Webster's (now owned by Watney) and Tetley, all at *The White Hart*. North-west along the B6107 one reaches the village of **Meltham**, where the Leeds-brewed Tetley at the *Traveller's Rest* can be recommended. Visitors to **Halifax**, almost due north as the crow flies, can enjoy both a visit around the ancient parish church with its curious poor-box effigy and a pint of Whitbread draught from the *Railway Inn*. Westwards, the A646 takes you to **Hebden Bridge** and to another Whitbread house, the *Fox & Goose*. Fans of English cricket will know of **Pudsey**, north-east of Hebden Bridge, where Sam Webster's beers can still be enjoyed on traditional draught at the *Park*.

Leeds is principally the home of Tetley, though some Younger's (Scottish & Newcastle) may also be encountered, particularly in old free houses like the *Old Unicorn* in Town Street. **Bramhope**, just north of Leeds, is worth a visit. I have enjoyed both a good pint of Tetley's bitter at the *Fox & Hounds* there and a snack in a pleasant though crowded bar. South of Keighley recommendations are needed. I would look for *The Bay Horse*—a Whitbread pub—at Oxenhope, which does good evening meals, and the *Royal Oak* in Haworth, a Webster house. The Brontë Parsonage museum is well worth seeing *en route* to **Stanbury**, a few miles to the west, where a good welcome is to be had at a Bass pub, the aptly named *Friendly*.

In **Keighley** itself Taylor's is the natural choice, for their beers have been brewed here for many years. *The Globe* in Park Lane and *The Volunteer* can be recommended for good local draught. The coal fire and the Leeds-brewed Tetley of *The Fleece* at **Addingham** on the A6034 from Keighley are an attraction, although you may prefer to travel to the village of **Cononley** beyond Airedale towards Skipton to enjoy Taylor's at the *New Inn*.

A walk across the moors and a visit around the 11th-century **Skipton** castle can give you quite a thirst, and the town offers several brews that include Whitbread (at the *Red Lion*), Tetley and CAMERON, the latter brought from County Durham. Many would prefer to travel the few miles west on the A59 to **East Marton** to enjoy a glass of Theakston's at the *Cross Keys*. THEAKSTON'S is a small family business which has been brewing since 1827; their own pubs only serve draught in a traditional way, but some of their free-house outlets now serve beer under extra pressure.

A day walking or driving up Wharfedale presents the opportunity of calling upon several inns of character. If you start at **Appletreewick**, north-east of the busy market town of Skipton, Theakston's Best Bitter can be enjoyed at the *Craven Arms*, while Tetley's is on draught at the *Forester's*

Arms in the attractive village of **Grassington**. Theakston's is also represented here at *The Black Horse*, and, a few miles north on the B6160, at *The Bluebell* in **Kettlewell**. At **Buckden**, the Old Peculiar, Theakston's slightly sweet draught is an attraction at the *Buck Inn*.

Farther west off the main A65 the Lancashire beer of Yates & Jackson may be found in **Ingleton**, which was once a pit village. The road to Ribblehead is fun if your car has good springs, especially after either the draught dark mild or well-hopped bitter of Yates & Jackson at *The Three Horseshoes* or *Ingleborough*, both at Ingleton. If you then take the road towards the cheese-making village of Hawes, where the Blue Wensleydale should be enjoyed if it can be found, you will pass through **Chapel Le Dale**. Here the aptly named *Hill Inn* serves good Theakston's.

Hawes lies under the bleak fells, a real tourist area, where Theakston's is to be found at the *Crown Hotel*, which has good snacks, too. East of here is the horse-training centre of **Middleham**. In fact, jockeys frequent the *Black Swan Inn* at Middleham, which serves a good pint of Masham-brewed Theakston's bitter. Northwards into Swaledale the A6108 takes you to the lovely old market town of **Richmond**, where you should see both the Norman castle and Theatre Royal. Two pubs serve traditional beer in Richmond: *Bishop Blaize* in the Market Square has Cameron's, while the one-armed landlord at *The Holly Hill Inn* serves Theakston's out of enamelled jugs.

Above Richmond lies a charming Dickensian coaching pub, the *Foxall Inn* at **East Layton**, five miles west of Scotch Corner on the main A66 road to Penrith. Here several beers may be enjoyed, but particularly Theakston's. Quite near is the Scots Dyke, the stupendous earthwork that extended at one time from central Yorkshire into Scotland, which is thought to have been the work of the local tribe, the Brigantes. West above Swaledale good draught Theakston's and splendid views may be obtained at the *C.B. Hotel* in **Arkengarthdale**.

Catterick boasts not only the famous military camp and good horse-racing but also good beer at *The Bay Horse*, a Theakston's house where your pint is pulled by a retired jockey. Just off the A1 try Theakston's Old Peculiar at *The White Heifer Inn* in **Scorton**. At the market town of **Bedale** with its charming wide cobbled street, the 16th-century

Oddfellow's Arms, tucked away in a narrow street called Emgate, also serves Old Peculiar. This pub derives its name from the masons who used to meet here. A few miles away at **Exelby** on the B6285 south of Bedale electric pumps have replaced the manual bar pulls at the early 17th-century *Green Dragon*. Webster's bitter as well as two Theakston's bitters are on draught; pleasant bar snacks are also served.

A few miles south lies **Nosterfield**, where the lovely handpumps enhance Theakston's Best Bitter which is pulled at the *Freemason's Arms*. Good snacks and overnight accommodation are also obtainable here, making it a suitable touring centre. Both this beer and William Younger's Scotch Bitter may be had on draught at *The Bruce Arms* at **West Tanfield**, just to the south-west. This is a fine spot for a summer picnic, especially for an open-air pint on one of the large stones in the middle of the River Ure. *The Bruce Arms* is a former coaching inn and has a most attractive interior. **Masham** is the home of one of the best traction-engine rallies in Britain, held in July, and provides Theakston's ales. This family firm uses no artificial additives in its beer other than flaked maize and should be applauded for the wooden barrels generally used.

Two Masham pubs serve Old Peculiar, the thirteen-bedroomed *King's Head* and the modern *White Bear*. Old Peculiar is named after the old ecclesiastical court of the same name, empowered to grant special licences. The beer is most attractive and slightly sweet. The *King's Head* has a dining-room within an 18th-century façade, but you may also like to try the beer in the tiny village of **Grewelthorpe**, which lies due south of Masham. There you will find both accommodation and a pleasant spot for dining at the *Hackfall Inn*.

Other villages around offering good draught ale are **Thirn**, just north of Masham, with the unusually named *Boot & Shoe Inn* serving Theakston's, to the west of Masham **Fearby**, where the *Black Swan* has the same good beer, and **Kirkby Malzeard**, with Younger's to be drunk at the *Henry Jenkins*; Kirkby Malzeard is noted for its cheese-making dairy. The market town of **Ripon** to the immediate east is well worth a detour, perhaps to see the magnificent west front of the cathedral, to enjoy good food at the Old Deanery or to drink draught Theakston's at *The Drovers* or *Magdalen's Inn* in Princess Road. I like *The Black Bull* on market day; try to catch the hornblower giving his message at nine o'clock each evening at a corner of the market place.

If you are touring within this lovely part of Yorkshire it is worth knowing that the village of **Copt Hewick**—just outside Ripon to the east—serves good Theakston's at the *Oak Tree Inn*, and at nearby **Pateley Bridge** at *The Water-mill*. Off the A1 one finds the *Punch Bowl Inn* at **Marton cum Grafton**, north-east of Knaresborough, serves the same Masham-brewed ale; so, too, does *The White Swan* at **Wighill** near Tadcaster.

York is an excellent centre for drinking traditional beer and visiting the famous Minster and the street known as the Shambles. Among the pubs to see are *The Cross Keys*, a Bass house in Deangate and Goodramgate, *The Acorn* in St Martin's Lane off Micklegate Hill, which serves the malty flavoured Cameron's Best Bitter, and *The Woolpack* in Fishergate, where the landlord serves a good pint of Whitbread's Sheffield-brewed Trophy bitter. If you are just outside York at **Sutton-on-Derwent** a good pint of Theakston's awaits you at the *St Vincent Arms*, a free-trade house of character. At **Huby**, a village off the A19 north of York, you will find *The New Inn*, a misleading name for this 500-year-old pub which serves good Younger's.

Actually on the A19 is the village of **Easingwold**, where you will find a welcome at *The George*, a Cameron's house with a good restaurant. Travelling northwards, the village of **Carlton Husthwaite** lies just south of Thirsk; here the *Carlton Inn*, known in the early 19th century as the 'Yorkshire Jenny', serves draught Cameron. A favourite pub of mine is *The Horsebreaker's Arms* at **Hutton Sessay**, which lies on the other side of the A19 from Carlton Husthwaite. This pub has a lovely collection of horse brasses and good bar snacks to accompany the draught Younger's. West of here the *Shoulder of Mutton* offers draught Whitbread and Younger's at **Asenby**; the village lies behind the inn on the banks of the River Swale. The cosy atmosphere is to be found here in a low-beamed, oak-panelled 'four ale bar' whose stone fireplace makes an interesting feature with its oven door and brass fittings of earlier days. At **Busby Stoop** near Thirsk the inn of the same name commemorates an 18th-century murderer who was hanged in chains on the gallows. The pub has a seat in its cellar, only recently removed from the public bar, in which in this decade four people have sat and subsequently died. None of this detracts from the good Theakston's on draught and the pleasant bar snacks.

Younger's IPA, brewed in Newcastle, is served at the *Whitestone Cliffe*, **Sutton**, which lies on the A170 east of Thirsk; the pub was built over three centuries ago; its name originates from the limestone cliff which towers above the secluded Lake Gormire at the foot of the Hambleton Hills. Furniture by the 'Mouseman' carpenter may be seen at the *Forester's Arms* at **Kilburn**: this may well be the antique furniture of the future, and certainly adds a dimension to the Tetley and Younger's beers on draught. There is a stone mounting block in the yard of the *Foresters* which is still used on occasion.

Towards magnificent Rievaulx Abbey lies the village of **Scawton**, where the *Hare Inn* partly dates back to the 12th century and has associations with the once flourishing Cistercian community only three miles away. The cow byre is now a lounge at the *Hare*, where both Whitbread and Theakston's Old Peculiar are served. **Scawton** is well situated for visiting Helmsley, Thirsk, the moors and coast. Several pubs of character are to be found in **Helmsley**, but two in particular serve traditional ale: *The Feathers* and *The Black Swan*. The public bar at *The Feathers* is quite a show-piece of stonework and oak beams, even though the building was erected less than twenty years ago. William Younger's is on draught at both these houses. Enjoy this beer at *The Black Swan* with a meal; specialities include breast of guinea fowl stuffed with pâté and served in a brandy and apricot sauce.

South-east of Helmsley lies the village of **Harome**, where the friendly landlord of the *Star Inn* serves Theakston's beer. South at **Hovingham** is the Duchess of Kent's home; this makes a good centre for journeying to both York and the Vanburgh residence of Castle Howard. *The Worsley Arms* at Hovingham again serves good Younger's bitter. Farther south, towards York, the village of **Sherriff Hutton** lies in the Howardian Hills. There Theakston's Best Bitter tastes particularly good at *The Old Highwayman*, an historic hostelry that lies within the shadow of the ruined 12th-century castle, a reminder of the rule of Richard III.

The road to the east takes one to the busy market town of **Malton**, a good centre both for fishing and country walking. The beers of Cameron's of Hartlepool can be enjoyed at the *Royal Oak*. These include a dark mild and a balanced Best

Bitter. Taking the A169 from Malton, you will find the *Blacksmith's Arms* at **Last Ingham** full of character. The village lies within the North Yorkshire Moors National Park. St Cedd, a Saxon bishop, founded a monastery here in 660, and today the free house, which dates from 1700, serves several beers, including Theakston's on draught.

Northwards on one of the small roads into the Moors lies **Rosedale Abbey**, where the *Milburn Arms* serves Cameron's Best Bitter. The Abbey at Rosedale is in ruins; the pub was at one stage the house of the Steward of the Priory. The tourist will find the ancient oak beams, Georgian fireplaces and antique furniture a fitting spot to enjoy Cameron's ale. East of Pickering at **Allerston** on the A170 towards Scarborough lies *The Cayley Arms*, where Charles I halted when travelling in disguise. Here Cameron's offer several draught beers which are usually dispensed by electric pumps. The Norman church and views from Allerston forest make the village well worth a visit. Farther east on the same road at **Wykeham** Younger's ale may be enjoyed at *The Downe Arms*, an old Georgian coaching house. The parish church here is, curiously, separated from its steeple.

Above Scarborough towards the Moors lies the village of **Hackness**, in many respects rather isolated. Theakston's beer awaits those who travel to *The Hackness Grange*, a country hotel in fine grounds, while Cameron's may be enjoyed within **Scarborough** at *The Angel* in North Street.

One of the lesser-known Yorkshire brewers is based in Hull: the HULL BREWERY COMPANY of Silvester Street. Much of the beer is pumped electrically and is not to my taste, but can be found at *The King's Head* in **Beverley** in Saturday Market and in the rather dilapidated *Railway Inn* at **Goole**. Three Hull-brewed draught beers are to be found: a dark mild, an austere bitter and a light mild. At **Heck** near Goole good beer is to be found at *The Bay Horse* in the form of Theakston's and within **Goole** itself DARLEY's ales at *The Cape of Good Hope* in Doyle Street. Darley's brew at Thorne near Doncaster and make two good draughts—IPA, which is their bitter, and a mild known as Darley's Dark.

The pubs of north Yorkshire are so many and generally serve such good ale that it is difficult to suggest where best to visit. **Goathland** on the north Yorkshire Moors has Cameron's draught beers at *The Goathland Hotel*, as has the *Hart* at **Sandsend** above Whitby. Younger's ales are to be

found at *The Jolly Sailors* in **Moorsholm** on the Guisborough–Whitby road which is now in Cleveland. This pub
was once a haunt of smugglers, and the gun room with its fine
collection of antique firearms is well worth a visit. At *The
Clarendon* at **Marske-by-Sea**, south of Redcar, Theakston's
Old Peculiar is available on draught and other Theakston's
brews are available at *The Anchor Inn* at **Guisborough**.

Back in North Yorkshire we should see the pubs around
Northallerton, the market town and administrative capital of
the North. *The Black Swan* at **Thornton-le-Moor** lies just
outside Northallerton; at this house Younger's draught is to
be found. Bass can be found at *The Revellers* in the village of
Yafforth not far away from Northallerton on the B6271. The
half-timbered 16th-century *Fleece* takes a great deal of beating
within Northallerton itself. This is actually the oldest building in the town and lies appropriately enough in High Street.
Old Peculiar is on draught from Theakston's, and good bar
snacks are to be had, while newcomers to the town should not
miss the 'Porch House' that was built after the *Fleece*. Race-
goers will know why *The Non Plus Inn* was so named in the
village of **Morton-on-Swale** near Northallerton, where
Theakston's draught is again to be found. *The Black Swan* in
the village of **Brompton**, just to the west of the A684 from
Northallerton, is another Theakston's house to visit.

The two other independent Yorkshire brewers are at
Selby and Tadcaster. The SELBY (Middlesbrough) BREWERY
started brewing again in 1972 after a break of almost twenty
years. They brew a strong draught, which is supplied to their
one tied house, *The Board* at **Howden**, a small market town
near Hull.

SAMUEL SMITH of Tadcaster claim to be the oldest brewery
in Yorkshire. They brew four draught beers; a Light Mild,
4X Best Mild, a Bitter and Strong Ale. They also have a
good strong golden ale in bottle, called Sovereign. Their
beers can sometimes be found in Northumberland and
Durham. Tadcaster is a noted brewing town, being also the
home of John Smith's Magnet Ales (now a Courage subsidiary).

CAMERON'S of Hartlepool, brewers of Best Bitter and
Strongarm, have already been discussed and their ales may
be enjoyed over much of the north-east. VAUX & ASSOCIATED
is another brewer of note, based at Sunderland, the schooling
spot of the Venerable Bede; their slogan is 'beers to boast

about' and their draught ales include Ordinary—sometimes known as Pale Ale—Samson Bitter and, where this is not on sale, Lorimer Best Scotch, a rich balanced ale. I would try these at *The Oddfellow's Arms* in Shiney Row, **Houghton-le-Spring**, or at *The Bird* in **Pelton**, south-west of Sunderland.

Sadly few of the beers made by the NORTHERN CLUBS' FEDERATION of Newcastle can be found in pubs, as they go almost exclusively to the working men's clubs; they can, however, be found in the bar of the *House of Commons*. The policy of stating the Original Gravity on the label has a great deal of honesty and is to be applauded.

In Northumberland Vaux ales are fairly easily found, such as at **Belford** in *The Black Swan*, while Cameron's can be tasted at *The Criterion* in **Hexham** and good Belhaven ale from Dunbar, Scotland, can be enjoyed at the *King's Arms* at **Berwick-on-Tweed**, a town encircled by its 13th-century walls. **Tynemouth** serves Whitbread at *The Salutation* in Front Street, as does also *The Star* in **Netherton**, on the B1331 west of Blyth. In **Blyth** itself Vaux keep good beer at *The Waterloo* in Havelock Street, and a few miles down the coast at **South Shields**, where the first lifeboat was built, Sam Smith's Yorkshire bitter may be enjoyed at *The Adam & Eve* in Ladygate.

CG

Scotland

Scotland, once the home of some famous beers, is now almost entirely lost to the big brewing groups, and it is very difficult to find any traditional draught beer. Scottish and Newcastle Breweries, Dryborough (Watney) and Tennent–Caledonian (Bass-Charrington) now have the majority of houses. But there are still three smaller brewers, BELHAVEN at Dunbar (previously known as Dudgeon), MACLAY OF ALLOA and THOMAS USHER of Edinburgh, a subsidiary of Vaux of Sunderland.

For those used to ordering bitter or mild south of the border, an explanation of the Scots equivalents will perhaps be useful. In Scotland draught or keg beers are usually called 'light' (a pale beer, alcoholically a little stronger than mild), 'heavy' (like English bitter) and 'export' (best bitter).

Dunbar in the Lothian Region provides a good starting-point for our exploration of Scottish beers. This attractive holiday resort with its derelict castle is also the home of Scotland's oldest independent brewery, BELHAVEN'S. The brewery was established in 1719, and has the slogan 'Proved by test, Scotland's best'. *The Eagle Inn* and the nearby *West Barns Inn* (on the A1087 towards Edinburgh) are good places to try their light ale, which has an original gravity of 1032. Between Dunbar and West Barns lies the *Mason's Arms* in **Belhaven** itself, where the heavy beer on draught can be recommended.

Edinburgh has a wide choice of pubs where Usher's may be found, but it is all keg on draught. By comparison, the natural heavy beer of Belhaven to be found in *Bennet's Bar* comes as a surprise. There are two *Bennet's Bars* with this excellent beer, one in Leven Street, next to the King's Theatre, and the other in Maxwell Street.

Draught Belhaven may be enjoyed at the Buckstone Lounge in Edinburgh's *Braid Hills Hotel*, in Braid Road, and at nearby Dalkeith. At **Dalkeith**, Newbattle Abbey is worth visiting; Belhaven draught can be found at the *Justinless Inn* at **Eskbank**, on the A7 to Galashiels. South of Edinburgh, with Scald Law (1898 feet) in the background, is **Penicuik**. Off the A701 near Penicuik, *The Howgate Inn*, which has a high reputation for its food, serves draught Belhaven, as does the *Old Grey Horse* at **Balerno**, a small village just off the A70 south-west of Edinburgh. Outside Edinburgh, at **Piershill**, Belhaven beer may be found at *Porter's Bar*, where the strong export may be drunk on draught.

Those driving between Edinburgh and Glasgow may like to make a detour to *The Cross Tavern* at **Whitburn** just off the motorway, or farther west to **Harthill**'s *Royal Bar*, again just off the motorway. In both these pubs you will find Belhaven's on draught. *The Drumclog Inn* in Todshill Street, **Strathaven**, also serves Belhaven on draught; Strathaven is on the A71 south of Glasgow.

In **Lanark**, near the Clyde, you will find Belhaven's at the *Port Vaults*; this is not a tied house, but the ale is well kept. North-west of Hamilton, known for its wild white cattle in the ruins of Cadzow Castle, stands **Cambuslang**. Good Belhaven brews may be drunk in both the *Sefton Bar* at 40 Main Street and at the *Toll Bar* at 56 Hamilton Road. Of the many bars to try in **Glasgow**, the *Auld Hoose* at Baillieston is worth seeking for a glass of Belhaven draught.

West of Glasgow at **Johnstone**, the *Stand Bar* in Houston Square serves Maclay's on draught. The brewer's sign is a green thistle on a white barrel. A small village, **Bishopton**, lies only a short distance away on the Clydebank–Greenock road, and serves Belhaven ale at the *Golf Inn*.

On the other side of Glasgow good beer is to be found from Maclay at the *Rowantree Inn*, Old Mill Road, at **Uddingston** on the A74, while a few miles to the north, *The Forge Inn* in **Coatbridge**'s Whifflet Street serves the same draught. Continuing north, Belhaven beers can be enjoyed at the *Railway Tavern* at **Caldercruix**; this town lies north-east of Airdrie on the A89. West of Falkirk, the town of **Denny** in the Central Region has Belhaven draught available at the *Royal Oak*, while the busy bar in the *Woodside Hotel* in **Falkirk** itself serves a good pint of Belhaven. It is a pleasant drive to **Kincardine** in Fife, where Maclay's beer is to be found at the *Bridge Bar* in Keith Street.

At the fine town of **Dunfermline** the *Dander Inn* at delightfully named Rumbling Well serves good Belhaven beer. The magnificent abbey, dating from 1702, with its royal tombs, including that of Robert the Bruce, should not be missed. A second pint of Belhaven ale can be had in Dunfermline at the *Old Abbey Tavern*.

Clackmannan in Central Region also boasts a good draught of beer—this time of Maclay's—at the *County Hotel*, 1–3 Main Street. West of here, **Alloa,** the home of Maclay's, has the same beer at the *Thistle Bar* in Junction Place, a particularly busy spot on the third Saturday in June when the agricultural show takes place. Maclay's brew three traditional draught ales. Pale Ale is their lightest, which can be found in practically all their pubs. Maclay's Export and SPA have a considerable following, and are often to be found in the towns, and less frequently in the country districts. You can find all three ales in many non-tied outlets, but usually dispensed under CO_2 pressure. Direct cask or compressed air are the two forms of serving normally found in Maclay's town pubs.

Just a few miles north of Alloa on the B908 lies **Alva**, where draught Maclay's can be enjoyed at the *Cross Keys Inn* in Stirling Street. Maclay's is also on draught at the village of **Menstrie**, on the A91 towards Stirling. The best bar in Menstrie is *The Hollytree* in Main Street East.

The popular resort of **Aberdour** on the coast of Fife has more to offer than castle ruins and sand; good Maclay's at *The Forester's Arms* in Shore Road. It is not far northwards to **Lochgelly**, where Belhaven ale is served at the *Central Bar*. The small village of **Kinnesswood** in Tayside is situated almost on lovely Loch Leven, and serves Belhaven beer at the *Lomond Hotel*.

Bonnie **Dundee**, with its University and attractive small zoo, houses two good Belhaven pubs. One is the *Ascot Bar* in Tay Street, while the second pint can be enjoyed at the *Bowbridge Bar* in Main Street. Still in the Tayside Region is **Arbroath**, where an excellent pint of Maclay's is served at the *St Thomas Bar*. Arbroath lies east of Dundee on the A92, and should also be seen for its red abbey, which is open between July and August, and for its sandy beach.

There remain two further outlets of good Scottish beer. They are **Dalmellington** in the Strathclyde Region, where Maclay's on draught is to be found in the High Street's *Snug Bar*. The other is the great seaport of **Aberdeen**, where Belhaven beer may be enjoyed at the *Dutch Mill Hotel* in Queen's Road, which I found to be the road out to Alford.

Mention should be made of the good bottled beer of *Traquair House*, **Innerleithen**, in the Borders Region. This beer is made in the 12th-century house which claims to be the oldest in Scotland. Since 1965 the old brewhouse has been in operation once more, and the proprietor is given technical aid by Belhaven Brewery.

CG

The Midlands
Warwickshire, Staffordshire, Leicestershire, Derbyshire, Nottinghamshire

Warwickshire boasts only one independent brewery, DAVEN-PORTS of Birmingham, who brew two good traditional draught ales, a dark mild and a flavoury fruity bitter. Their keg beers are called 'Drum'. In addition, throughout the Midlands you will find the Birmingham brews of Mitchells and Butlers (Bass-Charrington) and Ansells (part of Allied). Davenport's bitter can be found at **Napton** at the aptly named *Napton Bridge*, not far from Stratford-upon-Avon, while a few miles to the west of Stratford, Ansells may be drunk at the *Three Tuns* in High Street, Henley-in-Arden. The old timber houses in Henley remind one that this used to be an ancient forest town.

In **Stratford-on-Avon**, *The Shakespeare Hotel* features draught Donnington bitter from Oxfordshire in its 'Froth and Elbow' Bar.

If you take the A46 north from Stratford you will come to **Warwick,** with its 14th-century castle, whose grounds were laid out by 'Capability' Brown. Near by is the *Zetland Arms* in Church Street. This is a Davenport's house down a small side street that serves both bitter and mild from handpumps. The *Zetland* is a simple mid-18th-century house with a friendly atmosphere. The rooms are not luxurious, but breakfasts are recommended. At nearby **Kenilworth** Daven-port's is to be found at the *Virgins and Castle*. There is much remaining of the castle ruins, which should not be missed. The castle was the inspiration for Scott's novel of Elizabethan England.

Just north-east of Kenilworth lies **Leamington Spa**, famous for its concert pavilion and Royal Pump Room. Davenport beers are to be found at both the *Coach & Horses* and *Hope Tavern*. Many also enjoy the Mitchells & Butler's bitter at the *Red House* in Radford Road. A country pub by comparison is Ansell's *The Case is Altered* at **Fiveways** on the A41 between Warwick and Solihull; this is one of many pubs with this name, often reflecting a past change in licensee. Around **Birmingham** Davenport's may be tasted at *The White Horse* in **Sutton Coldfield** and at *The Boat* in **Solihull**.

Staffordshire is a fine county for brewers: THE OLD SWAN at Netherton, MARSTON, THOMPSON & EVERSHED of Burton, BATHAM of Brierley Hill, JPS, also of Brierley Hill, and the WOLVERHAMPTON & DUDLEY BREWERY in Wolverhampton itself. Of these Mrs Pardoe's Old Swan brewery must rank as the least known. The beer is brewed just south of Dudley on the A461 in Halesowen Road and served both there and at the *White Swan* in Holland Street, **Dudley**. A traditional draught bitter is made for both these outlets.

Better known is JPS Breweries of Brierley Hill, who have quite an extensive free trade apart from their seventeen tied pubs. Three traditional draught ales are brewed by JPS under the Simpkiss label. They are a dark mild, a richly flavoured Best Bitter and a strong dark, known as Old Ale, which is brewed in the winter months. Many of the pubs use a traditional manual bar pull, but an increasing number are moving over to electric pumps. In **Brierley Hill** JPS beers (the inn sign more often says 'Simpkiss') can be enjoyed at the *New Inn* in Dudley Road. Brierley Hill is also the home of brewer Daniel Batham, two of whose own pubs lie within this pottery town. They are *The Vine*, Delph Road, and the *Holly Bush*, Pensnett. Wooden casks are still used by this small independent brewer and their beer is served by handpumps.

South-west of Brierley Hill, **Kinver** lies just off the A449. Here JPS may be enjoyed in the High Street at the *Olde Plough*, which has a fine display of brass and copper. In the same village Batham's have *The Plough & Harrow*, while the Nottinghamshire-based brewers, HARDY & HANSON, have *Ye Olde White Harte*, a delightful pub with a real village atmosphere and children's play area.

In this area the signs of Banks and Hanson are quite frequent. These are the brews of the Wolverhampton and Dudley Brewery, Banks coming from Wolverhampton.

At **Bilston**, between Wolverhampton and Dudley, Julia Hanson's draught bitter and mild, a fuller beer than that brewed by its sister company Banks, can be found at the *Horse and Jockey* in Church Street. Quite fittingly for this centre of the coal trade, a roaring open fire greets you. The mild may be tasted at the oddly named *United Kingdom* in

Bloxwich Road North, at **Short Heath**, near the Wyrley and Essington canal. You may like to experience the sing-song at another Banks' pub, *The Chase* in Watling Street, **Brownhills**, on the A5, north of Walsall.

Marston, Thompson & Evershed are based in the famous brewing town of **Burton-upon-Trent**. The water in the town has been recognised since the mid-19th century as being ideal for the production of pale ales in bitter style.

No beer enthusiast's visit to Central England can be complete without a look at Burton-upon-Trent. If your visit is in May there is a regatta to watch also. Today home-made beermakers refer to 'burtonising' their water! In Burton good ale in the traditional draught style may be had at *The Victoria* in Horninglow Road or *The Albion* next to the Marston brewery. Both these pubs serve Marston's draught BB. By comparison, *The Blue Post* in Burton's High Street offers Bass Worthington's draught bitter. Marston's brew three draught ales: Burton Bitter, a slightly sweeter and stronger beer known as Pedigree and a dark mild. **Shenstone**, due south of Lichfield, is one point to enjoy the BB at the *Railway* in Main Street, although you can also try *The Gate* in the village of **Amington**, just east of Tamworth, with its fine 16th-century castle. A cathedral city steeped in history, also worth visiting for its beer is **Lichfield**, whose three graceful spires are known as the Ladies of the Vale. *The Angel* in Market Street serves the draught bitter of Banks. West on the B5012 you can try Banks' mild at *The White Hart* in Wolverhampton Road, **Cannock**.

In the splendid Cannock Chase to the north it is well worth searching out village pubs. I like *The Garth*, a Banks' house, just outside **Dunston** which lies north of the attractive village of Penkridge and close to junction thirteen of the M6.

Leicestershire has two independent brewers: HOSKINS and EVERARDS. The Everard's slogan is 'Gentlemen, the best' and their sign is a man drinking within a circle. Very few Everard pubs use handpumps, but generally not much CO_2 pressure is applied in their dispensing systems for their draught ales.

Leicester has *The Craddock* in Knighton Lane, an old thatched pub that serves Everard's Burton Mild, which is dark in colour; an older house, *The Shakespeare* in Braunstane Lane, dating from *c.* 1640, offers the stronger Tiger Draught. Marston's offer their beers at *The Fosse Way* in Melton Road.

East of Loughborough at **Barrow-on-Soar** I would

recommend the beers of Nottinghamshire brewer SHIPSTONE at the *Navigation Inn*. This is a canal-side pub where you can enjoy the well-hopped Shipstone Bitter while you watch the passage of the narrow boats on the canal. In **Loughborough**, Shipstone has another canal-side pub, *The Albion* on Canal Bank. Many also enjoy Everard's new house, *The Gallant Knight*, which, according to tradition, was built on the site of Knight Thorpe Hall. In Market Street I have enjoyed the bitter from Marston's at *The Griffin* and HOME of Nottingham's full, dark mild at the *Blacksmith's Arms* in Bedford Square. The beer here is drawn by handpump, and the pub is well equipped for games and the lounge has an organ.

HOSKINS of Beaumanor Road, Leicester, has only one tied house and it is therefore not surprising that its motto is 'have a drink at home'. The pub in question is *The Red Lion* in Park Street, **Market Bosworth**, near the scene of Richard III's death on Bosworth Field. From the outside it would be difficult to see whose beers were on sale, but in fact you will find two traditional draught ales, a nutty flavoured bitter and a dark coloured mild. In this area a number of free houses have Hoskins' beers.

Around Market Harborough Davenport's of Birmingham have several outlets. One place where their dark mild may be enjoyed is *The Harborough Lounge* in Church Street, **Market Harborough**. Everard's *Cherry Tree*, Church Walk, Little Bowden, in the same town makes for pleasant comparison, while you may like the rural atmosphere of *The Neville Arms*, a Marston's house in the village of **Medbourne**, which lies on the B664 from Market Harborough.

The traveller now enters what used to be the smallest county of England, Rutland, now part of Leicestershire. Here the fine brewer, RUDDLE OF OAKHAM, is based. Ruddle's make two draught beers throughout the year, Bitter and County. Of these beers Ruddle's County is the stronger. At **Uppingham**, noted for its distinguished school and good hunt, the *Exeter Arms* serves Ruddle's Bitter, while *The Crown* has the County on draught. I also rather like the atmosphere of nearby **Bisbrooke**, scarcely a mile to the east off the A47, where good beer may be consumed at *The Gate*. The County ale may be had on draught at Ruddle's *Noel Arms* at **Langham**, near Oakham, and both their draught ales at the *Sun Inn* at **Cottesmore**, which lies on the B668 from Oakham. Another village pub is the *Black Bull* at **Market Overton**, which has a party room, or the larger *White Lion* at **Whissendine**, both of which serve Ruddle's. *The White Lion* is well placed with both the Bitter and County on tap and a restaurant where you can enjoy some of the recipes devised by Rosemary Hanson, youngest daughter of Sir Kenneth Ruddle. A similar choice of Ruddle's ales may be found at the *Fox & Goose* at **Illston-on-the-Hill** in Leicestershire or at the *Queen's Head* in **Billesdon**. I like the *Golden Fleece* in **South Croxton**, which lies between Oakham and Leicester and where you can enjoy a good pint of Ruddle's County on draught.

It is then not far to **Syston** on the A607 north of Leicester, where you will find Shipstone's Bitter at the *Baker's Arms*. Further north, in the pork-pie-producing town of **Melton Mowbray**, home of Nottingham's fruity bitter and dark mild can be tried in the *Black Swan* in Sherrard Street. There may be a conflict of traditional ale loyalties in Melton Mowbray, for Ruddle's has an attractive outlet in the *Noel Arms*, with its County ale on draught.

North of Burton up the A38, turn off east to Willington across the county border to Derbyshire to *The Rising Sun* at **Willington**, near the Trent and Mersey Canal. This village pub serves Marston's ales, for there are no Derbyshire-based independent brewers. **Ashbourne**, a good centre from which to explore the beautiful Peak District with its summer well dressings, has good beer at the *Green Man & Black's Head*. Here you will find the Pale Ale of Greenall Whitley of Lancashire. North-east of Ashbourne, off the A524, Marston's traditional beers may be found at *The Gate* at **Brassington**, which has most attractive horse brasses. Off the A6 to the east at the village of **Crich** several pubs offer the Best Bitter made by Nottinghamshire brewer Hardy & Hanson. These include *The Cliff*, a stone pub not far from the Tramway Museum, and the *Black Swan* in the Market Place. In **Buxton** you may well have trouble in finding local traditional ale, but at *The Grove* in Grove Parade the Cheshire brewers Frederic Robinson offer their Best Mild. At **Ilkeston**, there is the opportunity to enjoy Sheffield-brewed Ward's ales at the *Durham Ox*, while the *Horse & Groom* has Shipstone's beer. The yellow hop sign of Hardy & Hanson's is to be found over much of this part of England, with its rolling country and fine parish churches. Hardy's are one of the four independent

Nottinghamshire brewers: SHIPSTONE'S, MANSFIELD'S, HOME'S of Daybrook and HARDY & HANSON'S of Kimberley. Hardy & Hanson's was formed out of the amalgamation of Robinson's—a Kimberley-based brewery which was established in 1832—the brewery owned by William and Thomas Hardy on the other side of the street, and Hanson's. The merger finally took place in 1972. Home's was founded in 1890 on the acquisition of John Robinson's of Daybrook. This company in turn purchased W. H. Hutchinson in 1914, George Green in 1921 and Killingley & Co. in 1925. Their ales are identified outside their tied outlets by a Robin Hood sign in green. James Shipstone founded his brewery in New Basford in 1852. With his son as partner, the firm expanded and acquired Carrington's in 1898, Beeston Brewery in 1922 and George Hooley four years later.

Nottinghamshire-brewed ales can be found in most of the surrounding counties. In Nottinghamshire itself, try Hardy & Hanson's at *The Sun* in **Eastwood**, a good spot to 'stop with the hop' as Hardy's slogan puts it; their Best Bitter, a well-hopped ale, is served in the traditional manner. **Basford** lies not far from Home's brewery, and here Home's ales are served at *The Barley Mow* in Basford Road.

The other pubs around give one the opportunity to try all this county's ales, and even those from neighbouring centres. Ruddle's County may be had at *The Windmill Inn* at **Redmile**, near Grantham, or at **Sewstern** at the oddly named *Blue Dog*. On the outskirts of Nottingham you will find **Burton Joyce**, where Shipstone's Bitter may be ordered at the *Lord Nelson*, or away in **Sutton-in-Ashfield** the *Duke of Sussex* serves Hardy & Hanson's beers. Few Mansfield pubs are to be found easily outside Mansfield, which lies on the edge of Sherwood Forest but which is more noted for its colliery and mills. Two draught ales are made by Mansfield's, a bitter and dark mild. I would taste them in the *Old Ramme* in Church Street, **Mansfield**, or at *The King's Arms*—a misnomer for a pub in this town—in Ratcliffe Gate. In all events central England offers a wide choice of good houses, lovely ales and splendid stories to listen to and retell around the welcoming bars.

CG

East Anglia
Norfolk, Suffolk, Cambridgeshire, Lincolnshire

The local independent brewers are GREENE KING of Bury St Edmunds, ADNAMS of Southwold, ELGOOD'S of Wisbech, BATEMAN of Wainfleet, TOLLEMACHE & COBBOLD of Ipswich and PAINE'S of St Neots, formerly in Huntingdonshire.

Norfolk is synonymous with the Broads, and a good starting-point is **Geldeston**. By boat, journey up the river from Beccles through tree-lined banks to enter a small cut to *The Wherry*, an early 18th-century pub, with a tearoom serving lunches and dinners, in addition to the excellent Adnams ale. Gaily-painted ornaments made from sea-shells, the work of a villager while away on a lightship in the North Sea, are sold here. By road the pub can be reached by turning off the A143.

Nearby **Norwich** has a Tollemache pub in *The Wild Man* in Bedford Street, a city where it is otherwise difficult to enjoy traditional draught beer. Norwich is well worth visiting for its 32 churches and undisturbed medieval winding streets and antique shops.

Towards the coast just west of the market town of **Aylsham** lies the chance of a good Greene King pint at the *Buckinghamshire Arms*, only a stone's throw from magnificent Blickling Hall. Adnams is also often available at this free house.

Other Adnams' beers may be enjoyed west of Sheringham at *The Maltings*, in the village of **Weybourne**, or farther west along the coast on the A149 at **Blakeney**'s *The Manor*. This is not far from Holkham Hall, the early 18th-century Palladian mansion which may be visited between June and September. Continuing west, the village of **Burnham Thorpe** boasts the birthplace of Nelson and the appropriately named Greene King house *Lord Nelson*. Although the vicarage where Nelson was born no longer exists, this inn still boasts the room where the most famous of English seamen gave a dinner for the villagers before he took command of the *Agamemnon* in 1793. The beer is cask drawn by gravity.

King's Lynn takes you towards Elgood's brews. The sign of an Elgood pub is a greyhound with a key in its mouth, and its two draught beers are a slightly sweet dark mild and a lightly hopped bitter. King's Lynn should be seen for its splendid civic buildings like the Custom House built in 1683. Five miles west towards Sleaford lies **Clenchwarton**, where you can enjoy Elgood's bitter at *The Victory*. It lies not far from the Greene King house of *The Crown & Anchor* at **Wiggenhall St Germain,** four miles south of King's Lynn. The pub stands by the bridge over the River Ouse and faces across the village green. The house dates partly from the 14th century, and the fishing in the neighbourhood is to be recommended.

South of King's Lynn lies *The Crown* at **Downham Market**, whose parish church of St Edmund has a fine timber roof and a 500-year-old font. This pleasant hotel has a comfortable old bar where the locals appreciate the Worthington bitter on handpump. The snacks can be recommended. A few miles west lies the Elgood house of *The Red Lion* at **Outwell.**

The Romans once tramped past **Castle Acre** (north of Swaffham) on the Peddar's Way. The 11th-century remains of the Cluniac Priory may be visited. A Greene King pub, *The Ostrich*, has rooms and good beer. At nearby **Gayton** *The Crown* is also a Greene King's house. The open fires and old Dutch tiles around the grate are most attractive, as are the oak beams, old china and silk pictures. *The Crown* stands back from the road near the church and was built about 600 years ago.

Bury St Edmunds is the home of brewer Greene King, who makes five traditional draught ales. These are Abbot Ale, a heady full-flavoured bitter, IPA and IA Light Bitters, a dark-coloured mild known as XX and a light mild, which is more popular farther south. Of the Greene King houses in Bury, *The Falcon* on the corner of Victoria Street and Risbygate and both *The Fox* and *Greyhound* in Eastgate Street on the left of the A143 towards Diss are worth visiting. Bury itself has a fine Abbey Church with a double hammerbeam roof as well as Angel Corner for clock enthusiasts. *The Nutshell*, a Greene King house, claims to be the smallest pub in Britain, measuring twelve feet by seven; here two rugger clubs squeezed in eighty-three players some years ago!

Towards **Newmarket,** the great horse-racing centre, is *The White Horse* on the A45, a Greene King pub, and at **Kentford**—four miles from Newmarket on the left-hand side from Bury—*The Cock.* In Newmarket itself is *The White Lion,* a Greene King pub on the A11 London side and *The Bull Hotel. The Bull* is a delightful place for a pint of Greene King's bitter, especially in the summer when you can enjoy it sitting under the umbrellas in the hotel's yard.

South-east towards Sudbury, but still in Suffolk, lies **Long Melford,** worth visiting for its perpendicular church, Melford Hall (a once moated Elizabethan manor house) and its pubs of character. The two to recommend are *The Swan* in Hall Street, which has fine and beautifully polished beer pulls for the Greene King ale, and *The Crown,* in the same street. The landlord of *The Crown* is an ex-actor, and he ensures that the garden is kept immaculate and Greene King's beer perfect.

The village of **Kersey** is reached by driving on the B1115 out of Sudbury past Gainsborough's House and turning off right through Great Waldingfield. At the top of **Kersey** stands the 16th-century timbered inn known as *The White Horse,* where Adnams is available. Prints of cricketers adorn the walls and the flagged bar is complete with cast-iron fireplace; all is in keeping with a quiet village like Kersey, which was known in pre-Tudor times for the manufacture of cloth.

Farther east, in **Ipswich,** *The Greyhound* in Henley road is close to the hospital. This inn is the first Adnams house to be found after entering Suffolk from Essex and London on the A12. It is a compact pub with three comfortable rooms. Ipswich is worth visiting in June for the Suffolk Tattoo and at any time to see the Grinling Gibbons' carvings on the pulpit in St Mary-le-Tower church.

Ipswich is the home of TOLLEMACHE & COBBOLD; they have been brewing here since 1746. One of their trademarks is Cardinal Wolsey; this famous character was born in Ipswich. Three traditional draught ales may be found: Old Strong, especially a winter brew, Best Bitter, which has a distinctly hopped aroma, and a dark mild. *The Butt & Oyster* at **Pinmill** near Chelmondiston off the B1456 south-east of Ipswich is an ideal Tollemache pub to enjoy these brews. Pinmill is a riverside hamlet on the banks of the Orwell. The name of the hamlet dates back to 1323, and the pub has been the haunt of both fishermen and smugglers many times in the past. At **Felixstowe** across the estuary you will find the *Little Ships* with a large public bar serving draught Adnams. Drama festivals are still held in the town in the spring and autumn.

North-east of Ipswich on the A12 lies **Wickham Market**, where you will find a 15th-century coaching house known as *The White Hart*, some five miles from Woodbridge. This is an Adnams house with real character. One of the bedrooms was previously a hayloft!

Orford is only a few miles east from Wickham Market. The village of Orford still houses the keep of the 12th-century castle, which serves as a landmark for those at sea. Sailing and angling are popular here, and *The King's Head,* a fine Adnams' house, serves oysters. *The King's Head* dates back to the 13th century, while the smaller *Jolly Sailor* in Orford is a 17th-century inn, believed to have been built from the timber of wrecks. The table in the public bar was used as an air-raid shelter in the last War. There is a bird sanctuary worth seeing at nearby Havergate Island where the avocet is known to breed.

Some Adnams' houses serve Tally Ho, a barley wine, on draught in the winter months. You may encounter it at **Snape** on the B1069 north of Orford, famous for its music festival and annual antiques fair. *The Golden Key* in Snape offers both bitter and mild, the latter with a fruity aroma and dark colour, on traditional draught, but from metal rather than wooden casks. *The Crown* in Snape has also Adnams; the peepholes that were used to alert the smugglers are still there, as is the Old Codgers room, where Benjamin Britten gained inspiration for a setting for Peter Grimes.

Aldeburgh was mentioned in the Domesday Book and was once a famous port. Its more recent history includes having England's first woman doctor as one of its citizens. Of the many pubs to choose from I would commend *The Mill*, opposite the 500-year-old Moot Hall; *The Mill* serves good Adnams' brews and has fine views of the sea from its leaded windows. *The Black Horse* serves Adnams directly from the cask, and at *The White Hart* in the High Street you can enjoy a game of darts and a glass of Adnams. Only a short way northwards on the B1122 out of Aldeburgh lie **Leiston** and, nearer the coast, **Sizewell**. Leiston is a small industrial town by comparison with the festival resort of Aldeburgh. Adnams is available at *The Engineer's Arms* in Leiston, and at

The Vulcan in Sizewell, with its splendid sign depicting Hephaestus, the Grecian god who presided over fire and was the patron of all who worked in iron.

On the main A12 Ipswich–Lowestoft road lies the village of **Kelsale**. Three houses, all serving Adnams' beer, are to be found: *The Eight Bells*, which was a farmhouse until 1937, the modernised and darts-playing *New Inn* and a converted cottage known as *The Rising Sun*. Cribbage is popular in the long bar of the *Blois Arms* at nearby **Yoxford**, where Adnams' draught may be enjoyed. Cockfield Hall, an elegant Tudor house, is set back from the Yoxford road; here the sister of Lady Jane Grey died while a prisoner. Another country pub in the vicinity is *The Bell* at Middleton, an Adnams' thatched-roof house in a dip on the edge of the marshes. The mild is to be recommended at the one bar of this low-ceilinged pub.

The kitchen bar of the *White Horse* at Badingham on the A1120 serves Adnams' bitter and mild directly from the barrel. It is an attractive pub with a grandfather clock in the saloon bar and grounds outside where a pint may be enjoyed in the summer months. Nearby **Peasenhall** has Tolly Cobbold on draught at *The Swan*, while those who like the atmosphere of a farmworkers' pub should visit *The Bell* at **Dennington** to hear the local Suffolk dialect over a pint of Adnams. It is not far from here to **Saxtead Green**, where you can see the finest post-windmill in the country. In character is the nearby *Marlborough Head* in **Saxtead**, where Adnams' mild is on draught.

A stop in **Framlingham** to see the magnificent church allows you also to see a former chapel, now known as the *Railway Inn* (though no train is now to be seen!) for draught Adnams. If you enjoy pub games, 'ringing the bull' is to be found at another Adnams' house, *The Bell* at **Bramfield**. In this game a steel ring suspended on a cord is swung from the low ceiling on to a hook secured to the wall. On the outskirts of the village is Bramfield Hall, originally built in late Tudor times and rebuilt in the 18th century.

Adnams' houses are to be seen increasingly as you near the brewery at Southwold. In nearby **Walberswick**, a centre for artists, writers and bird watchers, you will find two: *The Bell*, once thatched and still in character with its two log fires in winter, and *The Anchor*. At **Blythburgh** an Adnams' house, the *White Hart*, used to be a court house and at another time a smuggling inn. Try to see its early Tudor cellar and taste the excellent local seafood.

This leads you to the quiet town of **Southwold**, where the perpendicular church is worth visiting. Kent and Worcester hops and local malt are used for the Adnams' ales. These are not pasteurised, but conditioned naturally to obtain more flavour. They may be enjoyed at *The Swan*, where you should see the elegant early Georgian fireplaces, *The Crown*, close to the common, from where there are magnificent views out to sea, or at the *Lord Nelson*, an old smuggling inn where you can see the dormer window on the landing which was used for flashing a lantern out to sea to warn smugglers when the Excise men were about.

Country pubs north of Southwold worth visiting for real ale include *The Plough* at **Wangford**, with its 60-year-old plough heralding visitors to the Adnams' beer beneath its sign, and in **Wrentham**, the Georgian *Spread Eagle* and the *Horse & Groom*, both serving Adnams. The *Horse & Groom* is popular for its pub games—cribbage, darts and dominoes. The thatched *Queen's Head* in **Blyford** stands opposite the church, where contraband used to be stored when the Excise men visited the house! **Halesworth**, nine miles from Southwold, stands close to the River Blyth and in both the 18th and 19th centuries trading wherries plied between it and the sea. *The Angel* in Halesworth, built in 1543, retains its traditional charm and serves good draught Adnams. You should look for the humorous hunting prints and old insurance plaques on the walls.

Before Lowestoft you can enjoy pints at the *White Horse* at **St James South Elmham**, north-west of Halesworth, an old Adnams' house with oak beams. In the *White Horse* one of the settles is a former church pew. In **Harleston** *The Cherry Tree*, on the left entering from Diss, serves Adnams, as does *The Buck* at **Rumburgh**, a delightful pub decorated with Georgian advertisements; the nearby ancient priory was founded by Benedictine monks in 1064. Adnams is on draught at *The Fox* at **Shadingfield**, south of Beccles; this pub has an adjoining playground for children. Try draught Adnams, too, at *The Falcon* at **Sotterley**; *The Falcon* is a converted farmhouse over a century old, and provides beer drawn straight from the cask by gravity feed. At **Bungay** *The Fleece* also serves Adnams; it is only a few yards from the famous Butter Cross, the ruins of the 11th-century castle and the elegant church of St Mary. This pub was given its name because farmers used to display their produce on the steps around the interior. Today it is worth visiting for its beamed façade and basic 16th-century construction.

The yachting centre of **Beccles** with its annual regatta in August should not be missed for good Greene King on draught. This can be enjoyed at *The Loaves & Fishes*, a converted maltings that recently won an architectural award. I have seen Morris dancers in the courtyard of the pub, which adds character to an already interesting spot.

Cambridgeshire is the home of ELGOOD's of Wisbech. They make two traditional draughts, but are increasingly using top pressure. They brew a dark mild and a rich flavoured bitter ale. In bottle, Fenman, a strong pale-coloured ale with a delicious mellow flavour, is popular. In **Wisbech** itself enjoy these at the *King's Head* not far from the 18th-century Peckover House, well worth visiting. South-west towards Peterborough are the brick-built *Railway* and the *Black Hart* at **Guyhirn**, both serving Elgood's. Towards Peterborough a stop at Elgood's *The Black Horse* at **Thorney** on the A47 can be pleasant, for it is a small pub and has a friendly landlord.

March is a beer drinker's find, especially for enthusiasts of Greene King. *The Jack of Trumps*, Dartford Road, gives the minimum four pounds pressure per square inch to the casks, and the landlord is willing to show his unusual collection of bottles, including the reminder of the days when Ogdon's brewed in March. Other March pubs which serve Greene King's Abbot Ale on draught include: the *Prince of Wales*, Station Road, and *The Ship* in Nene Parade. I also like the *Coachmaker's Arms*, a Greene King pub, on the right-hand side after the main square, driving from Guyhirn, and the *Horse & Jockey* in Wisbech Road (also Greene King) for atmosphere.

In **Peterborough** sound Elgood ales are to be found at *The Royal Arms*, on the Wisbech road, A47. You will notice its attractive window boxes.

Several of the Bedford brewer CHARLES WELLS' pubs are to be found south-west of Cambridge and within the city itself. Several houses still serve their two draught beers either by direct gravity feed or by manual pumps. In **Cambridge** the *Elm Tree* in Orchard Street as well as the *Ancient Druids* in Fitzroy Street are worth visiting. Tolly Cobbold still serve non-keg at Cambridge's *The Mill*, which is best visited during term time.

South-west from Cambridge there are several country pubs serving good Wells beer. These include the *Jolly Butchers* at **Haslingfield** and the nearby *Hare & Hounds* at **Harlton**. The bar food at Harlton—as at nearby **Whaddon's** *Waggon & Horses*—is good.

At St Neots, in the former county of Huntingdonshire and now in Cambridgeshire, is the brewer PAINE. Their pubs have the company's lettering in light blue on the exterior walls. Paine's brew two draught beers, a dark Special Mild and a well-hopped Three Star Bitter. Unfortunately both these beers are served by top pressure, which tends to make them gassy. There are several Paine's pubs in the town, such as *Royal Oak*, High Street, and *The Engine and Tender*, Cambridge Street, though you may like to make comparisons by trying the good County ale of Ruddle's at *Greenacres*, or Wells' ales in the *Golden Ball*, Market Square.

At **Bolnhurst** to the west of St Neot's you will find Paine's Ales in *Ye Olde Plough*, and the same beer is to be had in *The New Sun Inn* at **Kimbolton** on the A45 just to the north.

Huntingdon boasts not only the birthplace of Cromwell but also the fact that Pepys went to school here; the Grammar School of that time is now the Cromwell Museum. In the town you can enjoy Paine's ales at the *Victoria Inn*, and just outside at **Brampton** on the A141 a good pint, though a shade gassy, may be had at *The Brampton Hotel*. At the small village of **Offord Cluney** Wells have a house worth visiting that provides both lunches and dinners; it is *The Swan Inn*, which is set back from the banks of the River Ouse. Two miles to the west, leaving Buckden Palace on your left, you will find Wells' ales at both the *Spread Eagle* and the *Falcon Inn* in **Buckden**.

Lincolnshire has one brewery in GEORGE BATEMAN'S of Wainfleet, who make two draught beers traditionally: a well-hopped bitter and a light mild. North-east of Lincoln lies the country town of **Louth**, where Bateman's may be enjoyed at *The Thatch*. Nearer the brewery and south-east of Louth at **Alford** there is the *Half Moon*, where you should not miss the gargoyles on the church. At *The Roebuck* in High Street, **Lincoln**, the Nottingham beer of James Shipstone may be enjoyed. Melbourn's used to be the county's other brewer, but they stopped production over a year ago and now sell Sam Smith's ales. These can be tasted at *The Golden Lion* in **Bourne** on the A151 from Spalding or at the *Five Bells* at nearby **Edenham**, which has a playground adjoining it.

Elgood's can also be found in Lincolnshire—at, for instance, *The Peacock* at **Sutton Bridge**, near Long Sutton, where the church has the highest, most perfect timber spire in the country, or *The Bell* at **Holbeach**, between Long Sutton and Spalding. Ruddle's draught bitter may be enjoyed at *The Reindeer* at **Stamford** and at the *Hurdler Inn* in New Cross Road, as also at *The Dolphin* in the same market town.

Ruddle's ales may also be enjoyed at the *Golden Fleece* in Sheep Market, **Stamford**, while the strong County brew from this Oakham-based brewery is on draught at both the *Millstone Inn* at **Barnack**, near Stamford, and at *The Fox & Hounds* at **Old Somerby**, near Grantham. Good draught bitter from Ruddle's is to be found at the *King's Head* at **Morton**, north of Bourne. Eight miles south of Lincoln on the A607 is also the *King's Head* at **Navenby**, where Sam Smith's bitter is to be found as well as Sovereign Strong Pale Ale in bottle, which is not at all sweet; the bar snacks and the restaurant are good here. Two attractive Ruddle's country pubs are *The Griffin* at Irnham, south-east of Grantham, and *The Willoughby Arms* at **Little Bytham** on the B1176, where the County ale is on draught.

CG

Home Counties North

Northamptonshire, Buckinghamshire, Bedfordshire

A land rich in manor houses, period furniture, traditional village greens, and pubs and medieval churches. Although today parts of these counties are referred to as the 'commuter belt', they retain a country charm despite their proximity to London.

Two brewers of independent status are to be found within the region: CHARLES WELLS of Bedford and GREENE KING, who have a brewery at Biggleswade. In addition, a former Watney brewer has established a small and thriving enterprise to make ale in the traditional way, trading as the LITCHBOROUGH BREWING COMPANY. In the national league Whitbread have a brewery in Luton as well as the old Wethered's brewery in Marlow, and though some signs mention the Aylesbury Brewery Company, in fact this is now part of Allied, suppliyng their 'national' beers.

Brakspear's Henley Ales are often found in the area, as at **Marlow** on the A4155, a delightful spot, where the *Clayton Arms* serves these ales from handpumps. This may be compared with another Brakspear's house—the *Prince Albert*—in **Frieth**, which lies just south-west of High Wycombe.

High Wycombe makes a good centre to visit pubs and to enjoy this birthplace of the furniture trade. The arcaded 18th-century Guildhall puts one in the right frame of mind to approach the *Wendover Arms*, a Brakspear pub on handpump, or to set out south of the town to enjoy this Oxfordshire brewer's ales at village locations. West of High Wycombe, off the B482, you will find the lovely village of **Cadmore End**, where Brakspear's draught comes directly from the cask by gravity at *The Ship*, as it does at the *Old Crown* in **Skirmett**, a few miles to the south on the road between Fingest and Frieth. Younger's is another brewer who is represented here at the *Bedford Arms* in the village of **Chenies** off the A404 Amersham–Watford road.

Charles Wells still brew traditional ale, and have remained independent since their first trading days in 1876. The water for the Wells' ales comes from the brewery's own well in north Bedford, and the barley is frequently purchased from local farms. Their output, currently some 55,000 barrels, includes two traditional draught ales: mild and IPA bitter. The villages of **Mentmore** and **Cheddington**, north of Tring, lie near enough to High Wycombe to enjoy Wells' ales. Mentmore has the *Stag Inn*, while Cheddington has the equally pleasant *Rosebery Arms*; both villages lie between Tring and Leighton Buzzard in Buckinghamshire.

At **Luton** to the east one can taste Greene King's ales, and see the Wernher art treasures at nearby Luton Hoo, open during April to September. I have enjoyed the Greene King ales at the *Bedfordshire Yeoman* in Luton's Dallow Road as well as at *The Fox* in Darley Hall. Hot and cold food may be had with their beers in both these pubs as well as at the *George II* in Bute Street, a combination of names that will delight the student of Hanoverian history! By comparison you may like to try the bitter brewed by Charles Wells at both the *White Lion* in Park Street or at the *Compasses* on Farley Hill.

Turning again to the villages, **Arlesey** in Bedfordshire lies just south of the A507 Stotfold road south of Bedford. Charles Wells ensure good IPA is available at the *Steam Engine* and also at the *Airman* at **Meppershall**, which lies directly to the west of Arlesey. On the other side of the A6 the locally brewed Greene King can be tasted at the *Sow & Pigs* in **Toddington**, which lies on the A5120 on exit 12 of the M1. The pints are brought from the cellar; comparison may be made with Wells at the same village at the *Bedford Arms* or *Nag's Head*. Just down the road at **Tebworth** a more 'pubby' local atmosphere is to be found in the *Queen's Head*, a Charles Wells' house.

If you are travelling towards Northampton on the A5 there are two good pubs off the road north of Leighton Buzzard; these are at **Potsgrove**, which lies not far from Woburn Abbey, and at **Great Brickhill** on the other side of the main road. Both the *Fox & Hounds* in the former village and the *Duncombe Arms* in the latter serve draught Charles Wells' beers. In the summer a pint in the *Duncombe Arms* can be taken outside into their garden. If you continue driving westwards towards Buckingham another Wells' garden pint can be taken at the *Robin Hood* in **Padbury** on the A413 into Buckingham. North of Bletchley *The Plough*, a Wells' house, is worth a visit in the village of **Simpson** on the B488, while on the other side of the M1 you can reach the *Sir Francis Drake* by leaving at exit 14 for the hamlet of **Gayhurst**, north of Wolverton. The pub used to be the gatehouse to a public school and is well furnished; the bars, although small, are welcoming with Wells' mild on draught. A more simple Wells' pub is the *Watt's Arms*, in **Hanslope** nearby, whose lively and interesting landlord keeps IPA on draught.

There are more Charles Wells' outlets as we approach their home town of Bedford. Two pubs that you might miss if you did not know they were there are *The Wheatsheaf* in **Bow Brickhill**, just east of Fenny Stratford on the B557, and the *Red Lion* in **Salford**, which lies to the east of the new estate of Milton Keynes, on the other side of the M1. If you would like both a good bar snack and a glass in the garden during summer, try the unusually named *Leathern Bottel* at **Wavendon**, on A5130 some three miles south-west of Salford.

Greene King have several pubs round Biggleswade, one of their three brewing centres. **Clophill** on the A507 west of Shefford has Greene King's *Rising Sun*, where you can enjoy a good meal in the restaurant as well as their light mild on draught. **Elstow**, virtually on the southern approach to Bedford, presents the opportunity to visit Bunyan's cottage, followed by a visit to *The Bull* in London Road and *Three Cups* in Newnham Street, both of which serve Greene King's ales on draught. By comparison you may like to try either the *Black Swan* in **Shefford**, on the road between Bedford and Hitchin, or *The Harrows* at **Cotton End** on the same road, both of which serve Wells' beers on draught. One house that lies in a seemingly almost forgotten village—**Old Warden**—west of Biggleswade is even plainer, but has a certain character: Wells' *Hare & Hounds*.

The *John O'Gaunt* at **Sutton**, north-east of Biggleswade, is conveniently close to the golf course, and provides Greene King on draught. The pub serves good food.

South of St Neots are two country pubs that I enjoy visiting: one is *The Cock* at **Gamlingay** (actually now in Cambridgeshire) on the B1040 towards Biggleswade, serving Greene King on draught, and the other is *The Red Lion*, a Charles Wells' house, farther down the same road at **Potton**.

If you enjoy a good meal over traditional ale visit the Greene King *Polhill Arms* in **Renhold,** just out of Bedford off the A428, or the Wells' *Crown Inn* at **Hail Weston,** just outside St Neots on the Kettering road (again just inside Cambridgeshire). In summer months good pints may be enjoyed with the children in the gardens of *The White Horse,* a Wells' pub in **Keysoe** on the B660 north of Bedford, the *Simple Jackal* just to the south at **Thurleigh** and at the *Three Compasses* in **Upper Dean,** three and a half miles west of Kimbolton. Both the last two serve Charles Wells' ales and from Upper Dean you can visit Kimbolton Castle.

On the A6 out of Bedford the pubs are predominantly Charles Wells' houses. The *Fox & Hounds* in **Clapham** attracts good custom for their draught mild as do the *Half Moon* and curiously named *Swan with Two Necks* in **Sharnbrook,** just off the A6 to the left. South-west of Bedford good pubs include Greene King's *Green Man* and Wells' *Royal Oak,* both in **Lidlington,** not far from junction 13 of the M1: *The Chequers*—a Wells' house—at nearby **Millbrook,** and *The Bell,* a Greene King pub at **Westoning** on the A5120 north of the M1 Service Area, are also pleasant pubs.

Towards Northampton you may like to call at *The Horseshoe* in **Lavendon,** a Wells' house. Paine's have *The Three Cranes* a mile away at **Turvey. Ashton,** off the A508 on the other side of Salcey Forest, houses *The Crown;* this is a pub kept by an ex-boxer, decorated with photographs and other mementoes, and with good Wells' on draught. As at the *Half Moon* at **Grendon,** on the other side of the A428, the playing of skittles and darts is encouraged. Wells actually sponsor two major darts competitions. The local game of skittles is not the bowling-alley variety, but a game largely restricted to Northamptonshire and Bedfordshire which involves the 'skimming' of 'cheeses'.

Near Ashton lies an attractive pub, *The Boat,* right on the Grand Union Canal by the Waterways Museum at **Stoke Bruerne.** *The Boat* is a small free house with skittles and M & B on draught as well as several keg beers. A typical village pub is *The Red Lion* at **Yardley Hastings,** just off the A428 Northampton–Bedford road, with a public bar with low beams and a good darts board as well as a skittles room. Another such pub is to be found at *The White Hart* at **Stoke Goldington** on the B526. Both these pubs serve Charles Wells' beers on draught.

It is delightful to hear of a new recruit to the world of traditional brewing, and Bill Urquhart is a case in point. As a former head brewer for Watney, he knows exactly what is required of a distinctive brew. He established the LITCH-BOROUGH BREWING COMPANY only recently, but already you can enjoy his bitter in the *Pirate's Den* in **Farthingstone**, *The George* in **Maidford** on the B4525 and at the small *Red Lion* in **Blakesley**, which lies not far from Towcester near Canons Ashby House. In **Towcester** you will enjoy Wells' bitter in the Pickwickian *Saracen's Head* near the parish church, which has a Roman paving in the crypt.

North-east of Northampton the village of **Mears Ashby** is appealing, and a refreshing pint of Wells' on draught may be had at the *Griffin's Head*; the village lies just off the A45, taking the left turn at Wilby. Only a few miles to the north is the friendly, and oddly named *Ten O'Clock* at **Little Harrowden**; in fact, Wells' is served for half an hour after this time! The village of **Brixworth** is another not to miss on the A508 Market Harborough–Northampton road; *The George* serves Wells' IPA by handpump.

Those who drive near Corby may like to know of two pubs supplied by the Oakham brewers, Ruddle. They are the *Shuckburgh Arms* in **Stoke Doyle**, just south of Oundle, and the *Royal Oak* at **Duddington**, at the junction of the A43 and A47, a convenient place to stop for a pint should you be travelling between Leicester and Peterborough.

CG

Appendix of Brewers and Pubs Mentioned in the Text

LONDON

BREWERS

Bass-Charrington Ltd.
Courage Ltd.
Fuller, Smith and Turner Ltd.
Truman & Co.
Watney Mann
Whitbread & Co.
Young & Co.

PUBS

Anglesea Arms, SW7 (Ruddle, Young)
Bell & Crown, Strand on the Green (Fuller)
Bishop's Finger, EC1 (Shepherd Neame)
Black Friar, EC4 (Bass)
Buckingham Arms, SW1 (Young)
Cardinal Wolsey, Hampton Court (Fuller)
Churchill Arms, W8 (Fuller)
Coach & Horses, Kew Green (Young)
Coach & Horses, W1 (Charrington)
Crane, SW18 (Young)
Crown and Anchor, W6 (Young)
Dive, SE1 (Ruddle, Theakston, S. Neame)
Dove, W6 (Fuller)
Duke of Cumberland, SW6 (Young)
East India Arms, EC3 (Young)
Flask, NW3 (Young)
Guinea, W1 (Young)
King's Arms, SW6 (Bass)
Master Robert, Heston (Fuller)
Olde Cheshire Cheese, EC4 (Marston)
Old Ship, Richmond (Young)
Pied Bull, SW16 (Young)
Ram, SW18 (Young)
Roebuck, SW3 (Courage)
Rose, EC1 (Bass)
Rose & Crown, SW19 (Young)
Rossetti, NW8 (Fuller)
Royal Connaught, WC1 (Charrington)
Star, SW1 (Fuller)
Sun, Richmond (Fuller)
Turk's Head, SW1 (Charrington)
White Horse, SW6 (Ruddle, Young)

SOUTHERN ENGLAND

BREWERS

Burt and Co., Ventnor, Isle of Wight
Gale and Co., Horndean, Hants
Harvey (Beard), Lewes, Sussex
King and Barnes, Horsham, Sussex
McMullen and Sons, Hertford
Rayment, Furneux Pelham, Herts
Ridley, Chelmsford, Essex
Shepherd Neame, Faversham, Kent

PUBS

Essex

Bardfield End Green, *Butcher's Arms* (Rayment)
Braintree, *Bull* (Greene King)
    Waggon & Horses (Greene King)
Brightlingsea, *Cherry Tree* (Greene King)
Chelmsford, *Ship* (Ridley)
Chingford, *Royal Oak* (McMullen)
Chipping Ongar, *Cock* (Greene King)
Clacton, *Black Bull* (Greene King)
Coggeshall, *King's Arms* (Greene King)
Colchester, *British Grenadier* (Adnams)
    Buck's Horn (Tolly Cobbold)
Felsted, *Swan* (Ridley)
Finchingfield, *Red Lion* (Ridley)
    Yew Tree (Ridley)

129

Great Dunmow, *Cricketers* (Ridley)
White Horse (Tolly Cobbold)
Great Waltham, *Beehive* (Ridley)
Six Bells (Ind Coope)
High Roding, *Black Lion* (Ridley)
Howe Street, *Green Man* (Ridley)
Kelvedon Hatch, *Shepherd* (Greene King)
Little Henny, *Swan* (Greene King)
Maldon, *Queen's Head* (Greene King)
Blue Boar (Adnams)
Carpenter's Arms (Greene King)
Swan Hotel (Greene King)
Newport, *White Horse* (Rayment)
Radley Green, *Thatcher's Arms* (Ridley)
Saffron Walden, *Axe and Compass* (Rayment)
Gate (Rayment)
Stansted, *Cock* (Rayment)
Dog & Duck (Rayment)
Ash (Rayment)
Thaxted, *Swan* (Rayment)
Wicken Bonhunt, *Coach and Horses* (Rayment)
Woodford Green, *Cricketers* (McMullen)

Hertfordshire

Barkway, *Tally Ho* (Rayment)
Collier End, *Lamb and Flag* (Rayment)
Furneux Pelham, *Brewery Tap* (Rayment)
Star (Rayment)
Hatfield Heath, *White Horse* (Rayment)
Hertford, *Salisbury Arms* (McMullen)
Much Hadham, *Hoops*, Perry Green (McMullen)
Puckeridge, *White Hart* (McMullen)
St Albans, *Farrier's Arms* (McMullen)
Blue Anchor (McMullen)
Sawbridgeworth, *White Lion* (Rayment)
Ware, *French Horn* (McMullen)
Widford, *Green Man* (McMullen)
Wormley, *Old Star* (McMullen)

Surrey

Claygate, *Foley Arms* (Young)
Cranleigh, *Leathern Bottle* (King & Barnes)
Epsom, *King's Arms* (Young)
Esher, *Bear* (Young)

Farnham, *Queen's Head* (Gale)
Gomshall, *Black Horse* (Young)
Grayshott, *Fox and Pelican* (Gale)
Guildford, *Two Brewers* (Courage)
Hindhead, *Woodcock* (Gale)
Horley, *Gatwick* (King & Barnes)
Leigh, *Plough* (King & Barnes)
Milford, *Red Lion* (Gale)
Ripley, *Ship* (Courage)
Shalford, *Sea Horse* (Gale)
Shere, *Prince of Wales* (Young)
Surbiton, *Waggon and Horses* (Young)
Thursley, *Three Horse Shoes* (Gale)
West Clandon, *Onslow Arms* (Young)

Sussex

Ardingly, *Avins Bridge* (King & Barnes)
Battle, *Abbey* (Shepherd Neame)
Bepton, *Shamrock* (Gale)
Berwick, *Cricketer's Arms* (Harvey)
Brighton, *Harrison's* (Gale)
Bucks Green, *Fox* (King & Barnes)
Chichester, *Cattle Market Inn* (Gale)
Eastgate (Gale)
Chiddingly, *Golden Cross* (Harvey)
Eastgate Inn (Gale)
Cocking Causeway, *Greyhound* (Gale)
Dragons Green, *George and Dragon* (King & Barnes)
Easebourne, *Rother* (King & Barnes)
Eastbourne, *Hurst Arms* (Harvey)
Terminus (Harvey)
East Hoathly, *Forester's Arms* (Harvey)
Hailsham, *Red Lion*, Magham Down (Harvey)
Hastings, *Duke of Wellington* (Shepherd Neame)
Prince Albert (Shepherd Neame)
Horsham, *Bear* (King & Barnes)
Dog and Bacon (King & Barnes)
Lewes, *Black Horse* (Beard)
Lamb (Beard)
Lower Beeding, *Crabtree* (King & Barnes)
Loxwood, *Onslow Arms* (King & Barnes)
Midhurst, *Angel* (Gale)
Patcham, *Black Lion* (Harvey)
Rottingdean, *Black Horse* (Harvey)
Tillington, *Horseguards* (King & Barnes)

Uckfield, *Blackboys* (Harvey)
Upper Beeding, *Bridge* (King & Barnes)
West Chiltington, *Elephant & Castle* (King & Barnes)
Withyham, *Dorset Arms* (Harvey)
Worthing, *Jolly Brewers* (King & Barnes)

Kent

Aldington, *Walnut Tree* (S. Neame)
Bells Yew Green, *Brecknock Arms* (Harvey)
Bethersden, *Bull* (Shepherd Neame)
Biddenden, *Chequers* (Shepherd Neame)
Brasted, *King's Arms* (Shepherd Neame)
Canterbury *Bishop's Finger* (Shepherd Neame)
  Shakespeare (S. Neame)
Chilham, *Woolpack* (S. Neame)
Chillenden, *Griffin's Head* (S. Neame)
Dover, *Lord Nelson* (Shepherd Neame)
Faversham, *Three Tuns* (Shepherd Neame)
  Castle (Shepherd Neame)
  Sun (Shepherd Neame)
Herne Bay, *Diver's Arms* (S. Neame)
Hernhill, *Three Horseshoes* (S. Neame)
Hythe, *Globe* (Shepherd Neame)
Lenham, *Dog and Bear* (Shepherd Neame)
Maidstone, *Fisherman's Arms* (Shepherd Neame)
Sarre, *Crown* (Shepherd Neame)
Selling, *White Lion* (Shepherd Neame)
Sutton Vallence, *Clothworker's Arms* (S. Neame)
Tonbridge, *Forester's Arms* (S. Neame)
Tunbridge Wells, *High Brooms* (Harvey)
Whitstable, *Four Horseshoes* (Shepherd Neame)
Wrotham, *Rose and Crown* (Shepherd Neame)

Hampshire

Alderholt, *Churchill Arms* (Hall and Woodhouse)
Andover, *Swallow* (Wadworth)
  Lamb (Wadworth)
  Angel (Marston)

Boldre, *Red Lion* (Eldridge Pope)
Brockenhurst, *Rose and Crown* (Eldridge Pope)
Chalton, *Red Lion* (Gale)
Curbridge, *Horse and Jockey* (Gale)
Havant, *Old House at Home* (Gale)
Horndean, *Ship and Bell* (Gale)
Itchen Abbas, *Plough* (Marston)
Longstock, *Peat Spade* (Gale)
Long Sutton, *Four Horseshoes* (Gale)
Lymington, *Angel* (Eldridge Pope)
Petersfield, *Square Brewery* (Gale)
Portsmouth, *Dorchester Arms* (Eldridge Pope)
Ringwood, *Crown* (Eldridge Pope)
Southampton, *Marsh* (Marston)
Southsea, *India Arms* (Gale)
Waltham Chase, *Black Dog* (Marston)
Wickham, *King's Head* (Gale)
Winchester, *Crown and Anchor* (Marston)

Isle of Wight

Ryde, *Castle* (Gale)
  Simeon Arms (Gale)
Sandown, *Commercial* (Gale)
Ventnor, *Volunteer* (Burt)
  Mill Bay (Burt)

SOUTH-WEST MIDLANDS

Brewers

Arkell, Swindon, Wilts.
Brakspear, Henley on Thames, Oxon
Donnington Brewery, Oxon
Gibbs, Mew & Co., Salisbury, Wilts.
Hook Norton Brewery Co., Hook Norton, Oxon
Morland, Abingdon, Oxon
Morrell, Oxford
Wadworth, Devizes, Wilts.

Pubs

Berkshire

Beedon, *Coach and Horses* (Morland)
Harwell, *White Hart* (Morland)
Hungerford, *John O'Gaunt* (Morland)
Hurley, *Red Lion* (Henley)
Remenham, *Two Brewers* (Henley)
  Five Horseshoes (Henley)

Sandhurst, *Wellington Arms* (Henley)
Steventon, *North Star* (Morland)
Twyford, *King's Arms* (Henley)
Wokingham, *Hope and Anchor* (Henley)

Oxfordshire

Bampton, *Jubilee* (Wadworth)
Banbury, *Reindeer* (Hook Norton)
Barnard Gate, *Britannia* (Morrell)
Binfield Heath, *Bottle and Glass* (Henley)
Bix, *Fox* (Henley)
Burford, *Lamb* (Wadworth)
   Royal Oak (Wadworth)
Chipping Norton, *Red Lion* (Hook Norton)
Crowmarsh Gifford, *Bell* (Morland)
Cumnor, *Bear and Ragged Staff* (Morrell)
Dorchester, *George* (Morland)
Ewelme, *Shepherd's Hut* (Morland)
Goring-on-Thames, *Catherine Wheel* (Henley)
   John Barleycorn (Henley)
Henley, *Rose and Crown* (Henley)
Hook Norton, *Pear Tree* (Hook Norton)
Howe Hill, *Jolly Ploughman* (Henley)
Iffley Lock, *Isis* (Morrell)
Longworth, *Lamb and Flag* (Morrell)
Nettlebed, *White Hart* (Henley)
Nuffield, *Crown* (Henley)
Oxford, *Wheatsheaf* (Morrell)
   Marlborough Arms (Morrell)
   Turf (Hook Norton)
Shiplake, *Plowden Arms* (Henley)
South Stoke, *Perch and Pike* (Henley)
Stanton Harcourt, *Harcourt Arms* (Morrell)
Stoke Row, *Crooked Billet* (Henley)
Thame, *Star and Garter* (Morland)
Thorpe Mandeville, *Three Conies* (Hook Norton)
Thrupp, *Boat* (Morrell)
Warborough, *Six Bells* (Henley)
Watlington, *Fox and Hounds* (Henley)
   Black Horse (Morland)
Witney, *Red Lion* (Morrell)
   Griffin (Wadworth)

Woodstock, *Queen's Own* (Hook Norton)
   Rose and Crown (Morrell)
   Marlborough Arms (Wadworth)

Gloucestershire

Beckford, *Beckford* (Davenport)
Cheltenham, *Cotswold* (Wadworth)
Cirencester, *Golden Cross* (Arkell)
Fairford, *Bull* (Arkell)
Fifield, *Merrymouth* (Donnington)
Ford, *Plough* (Donnington)
Guiting Power, *Farmer's Arms* (Donnington)
Lower Swell, *Golden Ball* (Donnington)
Moreton-in-Marsh *Black Bear* (Donnington)
   Wellington (Hook Norton)
Stanton, *Mount Inn* (Donnington)
Stow on the Wold, *Queen's Head* (Donnington)
Tetbury, *Trouble House* (Wadworth)
Tewkesbury, *Berkeley Arms* (Wadworth)
Uley, *King's Head* (Wadworth)

Wiltshire

Aldbourne, *Blue Boar* (Wadworth)
Amesbury, *George* (Hall and Woodhouse)
Badbury, *Baker's Arms* (Arkell)
Beckhampton, *Wagon and Horses* (Wadworth)
Devizes, *Bear* (Wadworth)
   Castle (Wadworth)
   White Lion (Wadworth)
Downton, *King's Arms* (Hall and Woodhouse)
East Knoyle, *Seymour Arms* (Wadworth)
Fonthill Gifford, *Beckford Arms* (Wadworth)
Marlborough, *Green Dragon* (Wadworth)
Melksham, *King's Arms* (Wadworth)
Pewsey, *French Horn* (Wadworth)
Salisbury, *Bell and Crown* (Gibbs)
   New Inn (Hall and Woodhouse)
Stoford, *Swan* (Hall and Woodhouse)
Sutton Benger, *Wellesley Arms* (Wadworth)
Swindon, *Baker's Arms* (Arkell)
   Noah's Ark (Arkell)
   King's Arms (Arkell)
Upper Stratton, *Wheatsheaf* (Arkell)

Wanborough, *Black Horse* (Arkell)
Winterbourne Stoke, *Bell* (Hall and Woodhouse)
Wootton Bassett, *Currier's Arms* (Arkell)

THE WEST COUNTRY

BREWERS

Devenish & Co., Weymouth, Dorset & Redruth, Cornwall
Eldridge, Pope & Co., Dorchester, Dorset
Hall and Woodhouse, Blandford Forum, Dorset
Palmer, Bridport, Dorset
St Austell Brewery, St Austell, Cornwall

PUBS

Dorset

Abbotsbury, *Ilchester Arms* (Devenish)
Beaminster, *Greyhound* (Palmer)
Bishop's Caundle, *White Hart* (Hall and Woodhouse)
Blandford Forum, *Badger* (Hall and Woodhouse)
  Crown (Hall and Woodhouse)
  Three Choughs (Hall and Woodhouse)
  White Hart (Gibbs)
Blandford St Mary, *Stour Inn* (Hall and Woodhouse)
Bournemouth, *South Western* (Eldridge Pope)
Bridport, *Crown* (Palmer)
  Old Greyhound (Devenish)
  Swan (Palmer)
Buckland Newton, *Royal Oak* (Hall and Woodhouse)
Cerne Abbas, *New Inn* (Eldridge Pope)
Chideock, *George* (Palmer)
Corfe Mullen, *Coventry Arms* (Devenish)
Dorchester, *Trumpet Major* (Eldridge Pope)
  Goldie's Bars (Eldridge Pope)
  Plume of Feathers (Devenish)
  White Hart (Hall and Woodhouse)
  King's Arms (Devenish)
Fontmell Magna, *Crown* (Hall and Woodhouse)
Gillingham, *Phoenix* (Hall and Woodhouse)
Kingston Matravers, *Scott Arms* (Devenish)

Langton Herring, *Elm Tree* (Devenish)
Loders, *Farmer's Arms* (Palmer)
Lyme Regis, *Pilot Boat* (Palmer)
  Cobb Arms (Palmer)
Milton Abbey, *Hambro Arms* (Devenish)
Piddletrenthide, *European Inn* (Eldridge Pope)
  Green Dragon (Devenish)
Poole, *Guildhall Tavern* (Devenish)
  Pure Drop (Eldridge Pope)
Powerstock, *Three Horseshoes* (Palmer)
Puddletown, *Prince of Wales* (Hall and Woodhouse)
Reforne, *George* (Devenish)
Shaftesbury, *Crown* (Hall and Woodhouse)
  King's Arms (Hall and Woodhouse)
  Mitre (Eldridge Pope)
  Ship (Hall and Woodhouse)
Sherborne, *Antelope* (Hall and Woodhouse)
  Britannia (Hall and Woodhouse)
  Black Horse (Eldridge Pope)
Sixpenny Handley, *Roebuck* (Hall and Woodhouse)
Sturminster Newton, *Bull* (Hall and Woodhouse)
Swanage, *Mowlen* (Hall and Woodhouse)
Tarrant Gunville, *Bugle Horn* (Hall and Woodhouse)
Uploders, *Crown* (Palmer)
West Bay, *Bridport Arms* (Palmer)
West Lulworth, *Castle* (Devenish)
Weymouth, *Black Dog* (Devenish)
  Sailor's Return (Devenish)
  Market House (Eldridge Pope)
  Portland Railway (Hall and Woodhouse)
  Queen's (Eldridge Pope)
Wimborne, *Cricketer's Arms* (Devenish)
  Dorset House (Hall and Woodhouse)
  Oddfellow's Arms (Hall and Woodhouse)
  White Hart (Eldridge Pope)

Somerset

Castle Cary, *Clarence* (Wadworth)
Crewkerne, *Swan* (Devenish)
  White Hart (Eldridge Pope)
  Queen's (Palmer)
East Chinnock, *Portman Arms* (Eldridge Pope)

Holton, *Old Inn* (Hall and Woodhouse)

Lydford on Fosse, *Lydford* (Eldridge Pope)

Marston Magna, *Red Lion* (Eldridge Pope)

Norton St Philip, *George* (Wadworth)

Nunney, *Theobald Arms* (Hall and Woodhouse)

Penselwood, *Queen's Head* (Hall and Woodhouse)

Priddy, *Miner's Arms* (Home Brew)

Upton Noble, *Lamb* (Wadworth)

Wincanton, *Nog Inn* (Hall and Woodhouse)

Woolverton, *Red Lion* (Wadworth)

Yeovil, *Three Choughs* (Eldridge Pope)

Avon

Bath, *Angel* (Gibbs)
Cœur de Lion (Devenish)
Curfew (Wadworth)

Blagdon, *New Inn* (Wadworth)

Bristol, *Bay Horse* (Davenport)
Phoenix (Wadworth)

Clevedon, *Regent* (Hall and Woodhouse)

Priddy, *Miner's Arms* (Home Brew)

Redhill, *Bungalow* (Wadworth)

Weston super Mare, *Long John Silver*, Kewstoke (Wadworth)

Winford, *Crown* (Wadworth)

Devon

Axminster, *Axminster* (Palmer)
Millwey (Palmer)

Axmouth, *Ship* (Devenish)

Barnstaple, *Golden Lion Tap* (Devenish)
Golden Fleece (Devenish)

Bowd, *Bowd Inn* (Devenish)

Exeter, *Valiant Soldier* (Devenish)
Ropemaker's Arms (Devenish)
Great Western (Bass)

Exminster, *Royal Oak* (Devenish)

Exmouth, *Bicton* (Devenish)

Hawkchurch, *Old Inn* (Devenish)

Honiton, *White Lion* (Devenish)

Ide, *Huntsman* (Devenish)

Kilmington, *New Inn* (Palmer)

Kingsbridge, *King's Arms* (Wadworth)

Otterton, *King's Arms* (Devenish)

Ottery St Mary, *King's Arms* (Devenish)

Sidmouth, *Marine* (Devenish)

Slapton, *Tower* (Wadworth)

Topsham, *Bridge* (Wadworth)

Whimple, *New Fountain* (Devenish)

Withycombe Raleigh, *Holly Tree* (Devenish)

Cornwall

Bodmin, *Barley Sheaf* (St Austell)
George & Dragon (St Austell)
Duke of Cornwall (Devenish)

Breage, *Queen's Arms* (Devenish)

Bude, *Globe* (St Austell)

Camelford, *Darlington* (St Austell)
Mason's Arms (St Austell)

Delabole, *Bottle & Chisel* (St Austell)

Falmouth, *Mason's Arms* (St Austell)
Grapes (Devenish)

Fowey, *Riverside* (St Austell)
Lugger (St Austell)

Gweek, *Gweek Inn* (Devenish)

Helford, *Shipwright's Arms* (Devenish)

Helston, *Blue Anchor* (Home Brew)
Rodney (St Austell)

Launceston, *Eliot Arms* (Devenish)

Liskeard, *Barley Sheaf* (St Austell)
Railway (Devenish)

Looe, *Ship* (St Austell)
Double Decker (St Austell)

Lostwithiel, *King's Arms* (St Austell)
Globe (St Austell)
Monmouth (Devenish)

Mousehole, *Ship* (St Austell)

Newquay, *Red Lion* (Devenish)
Victoria Bars (St Austell)

Padstow, *Harbour* (St Austell)
Golden Lion (Devenish)

Penzance, *Crown* (Devenish)
Yacht (St Austell)

Perranarworthal, *Norway* (Devenish)

Polruan, *Russell* (St Austell)

Probus, *Hawker's Arms* (St Austell)

Redruth, *Red Lion* (Devenish)
Railway (St Austell)

St Austell, *Sun* (St Austell)

St Ives, *Castle* (Devenish)
Lifeboat (St Austell)

St Kew, *St Kew Inn* (St Austell)

Truro, *Barley Sheaf* (Devenish)
Market Inn (Devenish)
Star (St Austell)

Wadebridge, *Swan* (St Austell)

WALES AND THE BORDERS

BREWERS

Border Breweries, Wrexham
Brain's, Cardiff
Buckley's, Llanelli
Felinfoel Brewery, Llanelli
Greenall Whitley, Wem

PUBS

Hereford and Worcester

Almeley, *Bells* (Marston)
Bewdley, *Buttonoak* (Banks)
   Talbot (Davenport)
Bromyard, *Hop Pole* (Marston)
   Bay Horse (M and B)
Broadwas on Teme, *Royal Oak*
   (Marston)
Broadwaters, *Old Bear* (Banks)
   Hare and Hounds (Batham)
Castle Hill, *Mason's Arms* (Banks)
Chaddesley Corbett, *Swan*
   (Batham)
   Talbot (Hanson)
Cutnall Green, *New Inn* (Marston)
Droitwich Spa, *Star and Garter*
   (Davenport)
Eardisland, *White Swan* (Marston)
Elmley Castle, *Queen Elizabeth*
   (Marston)
Great Malvern, *Red Lion*
   (Marston)
Hay on Wye, *Three Tuns*
   (Mitchells and Butlers)
Hereford, *Cock of Tupsley*
   (Banks)
Kidderminster, *Land Oak* (Banks)
Kington, *Burton Arms* (Ansell)
   Royal Oak (Marston)
Ledbury, *Feathers* (Whitbread)
   Olde Talbot (Ansell)
Lyonshall, *Royal George*
   (Whitbread)
Ross on Wye, *King Charles II*
   (Bass)
   Man of Ross (Whitbread)
Shenstone, *Plough* (Batham)
Tenbury Wells, *Royal Oak*
   (Banks)
Titley, *Stag Inn* (Mitchells and
   Butlers)
Worcester, *Cardinal's Hat*
   (Davenport)
   Eagle Vaults (M and B)
   Red Lion (Marston)
   Star Hotel (Banks)
   King's Head (Banks)
Wychbold, *Crown* (Banks)

Shropshire

Bayston Hill, *Beeches* (Banks)
Bishop's Castle, *Five Tuns* (Home
   Brew)
   Black Lion (Greenall Whitley)
Cheswardine *Red Lion* (Marston)
Church Stretton, *King's Arms*
   (Greenall Whitley)
Cleobury Mortimer, *Old Lion*
   (Banks)
Coalbrookdale, *Valley Hotel*
   (Greenall Whitley)
Craven Arms, *Stokesay Castle*
   (Davenport)
Ellesmere, *Black Lion* (Border)
   White Hart (Border)
Goldstone, *Wharf Tavern*
   (Thwaites)
Hadley, *Summer House* (Marston)
Hinstock, *Four Crosses* (Marston)
Hopton Wafers, *Crown*
   (Davenport)
Jackfield, *The Boat* (Banks)
Leegomery, *Malt Shovel* (Marston)
Ludlow, *Feathers* (Whitbread)
   Rose and Crown Hotel (Greenall
   Whitley)
   Keysell's Counting House
   (Greenall Whitley)
Madeley, *All Nations* (Home
   Brew)
Market Drayton, *King's Arms*
   (Marston)
   Stormy Petrel (Banks)
Marton, *Sun Inn* (Burtonwood)
Oswestry, *Cross Keys* (Border)
   Fox Inn (Border)
   Unicorn (Banks)
Shrewsbury, *Britannia* (Greenall
   Whitley)
   Peacock (Border)
   Plough (Greenall Whitley)
   Charles Darwin (Banks)
   Unicorn (Greenall Whitley)
Whitchurch, *Victoria Hotel*
   (Burtonwood)
Whittington, *Penrhos Arms*
   (Border)
   Ye Olde Boot (Robinson)

North Wales

Abergele, *Cambrian* (Marston)
Bala, *Goat* (Border)
   White Lion Royal (Greenall
   Whitley)
Bangor, *Castle* (Burtonwood)
   Antelope (Greenall Whitley)
Beaumaris, *White Lion*
   (Burtonwood)
   George and Dragon (Robinson)

Bwlch y Cibau, *Cross Keys*
(Border)
Caernarfon, *Albert* (Greenall
Whitley)
Anglesey Arms (Marston)
Ship & Castle (Burtonwood)
Chirk, *Hand* (Border)
Dolgellau, *Stag* (Burtonwood)
Gledrid, *New Inn* (Banks)
Harlech, *Queens* (Greenall
Whitley)
Holyhead, *Albert Vaults*
(Burtonwood)
Prince of Wales (Greenall
Whitley)
Llanarman, *Raven* (Burtonwood)
Llanbedrog, *Ship* (Burtonwood)
Llanbedr, *Victoria* (Robinson)
Llanyblodwel, *Horseshoe* (Border)
Llandudno, *Alexandra* (Burton-
wood)
Albert (Greenall Whitley)
Llanfair Talhaiarn, *Black Lion*
(Robinson)
Llangollen, *Grapes Hotel*
(Burtonwood)
Smithfield (Border)
Bridge End Hotel (Robinson)
Machynlleth, *White Lion* (Banks)
Menai Bridge, *Four Crosses*
(Robinson)
Moelfre, *Kinmel Arms* (Robinson)
Mold, *Black Lion* (Burtonwood)
Cross Keys (Border)
Montgomery, *Bricklayer's Arms*
(Burtonwood)
Nant Peris, *Vaynol Arms*
(Robinson)
Newtown, *Pheasant* (Burtonwood)
Castle Vaults (Border)
Overton Bridge, *Cross Foxes*
(Border)
Penmaenmawr, *Fairy Glen Hotel*
(Marston)
Pentraeth, *Panton Arms*
(Burtonwood)
Ruthin, *Wynnstay Arms*
(Burtonwood)
Wine Vaults (Robinson)
St Asaph, *Kinmel Arms* (Greenall
Whitley)
Talybont, *White Lion* (Banks)
Talysarn, *Nantle Vale* (Marston)
Trefeglwys, *Red Lion* (Border)
Tremeirchion, *Salusbury Arms*
(Greenall Whitley)
Welshpool, *Crown Inn*
(Burtonwood)
Wrexham, *Horns* (Border)
Nag's Head (Border)
Old Swan (Border)

Mid Wales

Aberystwyth *Downie's Vaults*
(Banks)
Brecon, *Wellington Hotel*
(Worthington)
Builth Wells, *White Horse* (Welsh)
Crickowell, *Beaufort Arms*
(Davenport)
Gladestry, *Royal Oak* (Welsh)
Llanfihangel-nant-Melan, *Forest
Inn* (Mitchells and Butlers)

South Wales

Abergavenny, *Station Hotel*
(Davenport)
Ammanford, *Plough and Harrow*
(Buckley)
Cardiff, *Albert* (Brain)
Cardiff Cottage (Brain)
Carmarthen, *Drover's Arms*
(Felinfoel)
Cwmbran, *Blinkin' Owl* (Brain)
Kidwelly, *Mason's Arms*
(Felinfoel)
Llandaff, *Black Lion* (Brain)
Llanelli, *Stradey Arms* (Buckley)
Llannon, *Red Lion* (Felinfoel)
Newton, *Jolly Sailor* (Brain)
Pembrey, *Ashburnham* (Buckley)
Pendine, *Beach Hotel* (Buckley)
Penygroes, *Norton Arms*
(Felinfoel)
Porthcawl, *Pier* (Brain)
St Brides Wentloog, *Church House*
(Brain)
St Clears, *Penyrheol Tavern*
(Felinfoel)
Swansea, *Adam and Eve* (Brain)
Cooper's Arms (Buckley)

NORTH-WEST

BREWERS

Boddington, Manchester
Matthew Brown, Blackburn
Burtonwood, Warrington
Castletown Brewery, Castletown,
Isle of Man
Cumbria Brewers, Workington
(previously Workington
Brewery)
Greenall Whitley, Warrington
Hartleys, Ulverston
Higsons, Liverpool
Joseph Holt, Cheetham, Man-
chester
Jennings Bros, Cockermouth
Mitchells, Lancaster
Okell, Douglas, Isle of Man

Oldham Brewery, Oldham
Frederic Robinson, Stockport
Daniel Thwaites, Blackburn
Yates and Jackson, Lancaster

PUBS

Cheshire

Adlington, *Miner's Arms*
  (Boddington)
Alderley Edge, *Moss Rose*
  (Robinson)
Astbury, *Egerton Arms* (Robinson)
Bollington, *Holly Bush* (Robinson)
Chester, *Bull & Stirrup* (Higsons)
  Griffin (Holt)
Church Lawton, *Red Bull*
  (Robinson)
Cotebrook, *Alveney Arms*
  (Robinson)
Crewe, *Spread Eagle* (Greenall
  Whitley)
Gawsforth, *Harrington Arms*
  (Robinson)
Gurnett, *Old King's Head*
  (Burtonwood)
Haslington, *Hawk Inn* (Robinson)
High Lane, *Bull's Head*
  (Boddington)
Macclesfield, *British Flag*
  (Robinson)
Newbold, *Horseshoe* (Robinson)
Poynton, *Bull's Head* (Boddington)
  Farmer's Arms (Robinson)
Prestbury, *Legh Arms* (Robinson)
Smallwood, *Legs of Man*
  (Robinson)
Sutton, *Albion* (Robinson)
  Church House (Boddington)
  Traveller's Rest (Robinson)
Tarporley, *Rising Sun* (Robinson)
Tiverton, *Crown* (McEwan)
Warrington (Lancs), *Royal Oak*
  (Greenall Whitley)

Greater Manchester

Bolton (Lancs), *Prince William*
  (Boddington)
Bury (Lancs), *Sir Robert Peel*
  (Boddington)
Cheadle (Lancs), *Griffin* (Holts)
  Printer's Arms (Robinson)
  Royal Oak (Robinson)
Cheadle Hulme, *Church Inn*
  (Robinson)
Denton, *Chapel Inn* (Robinson)
  Fletcher's Arms (Robinson)
  Lowe's Inn (Boddington)
Failsworth, *Church Inn* (Robinson)
  Lamb (Boddington)

Hollinwood, *Smut Inn*
  (Boddington)
Marple, *Navigation Hotel*
  (Robinson)
Oldham, *Bath* (Oldham Brewery)
Rochdale, *Brunswick* (Thwaites)
  Hare and Hounds (Boddington)
Romiley, *Forester's Arms*
  (Boddington)
  Friendship Inn (Robinson)
Salford, *Wellington* (Holt)
Shaw, *Blue Bell* (Robinson)
Worsley, *Bridgewater Hotel*
  (Boddington)

Merseyside

Burtonwood, *Elm Tree* (Burton-
  wood)
Liverpool, *Crow's Nest* (Higson)
  Grapes (Higson)
  Wheatsheaf (Higson)
Prescot, *Hare & Hounds* (Higson)
St Helens, *Prince of Wales*
  (Burtonwood)
  The Talbot (Boddington)

Lancashire

Bamber Bridge, *Ye Old Hob Inn*
  (Brown)
Blacksnape, *Red Lion* (Burton-
  wood)
Brindle, *Lord Nelson* (Brown)
Cadishead, *Coach & Horses*
  (Boddington)
Clayton le Dale, *Bonny Inn*
  (Thwaites)
Croft, *Plough* (Greenall Whitley)
Fleetwood, *Mount* (Boddington)
Freckleton, *Ship* (Boddington)
Galgate, *Green Dragon* (Yates and
  Jackson)
Garstang, *Eagle & Child* (Brown)
Hest Bank, *Hest Bank Hotel*
  (Boddington)
Lancaster, *Ring O'Bells* (Mitchell)
  Sun (Yates and Jackson)
  Tramway (Mitchell)
  White Lion (Yates and Jackson)
Lathom, *Ring O'Bells* (Higson)
Ormskirk, *Yew Tree* (Higson)
Overton, *Ship* (Yates and Jackson)
Preston, *Moorbrook* (Thwaites)
  Old Black Bull (Boddington)
  Spindelmaker's Arms (Thwaites)
Slaidburn, *Hark to Bounty*
  (Thwaites)
Southport, *Guest House* (Higson)
Tarleton, *Legh Arms* (Higson)
Up Holland, *Plough & Harrow*
  (Boddington)

Walton le Dale, *White Bull* (Boddington)
Warton, *West View* (Boddington)
Wrea Green, *Grapes* (Boddington)
Wrightington, *Scarsbrick Arms* (Burtonwood)

Cumbria

Bowness on Windermere, *Albert* (Hartley)
New Hall (Hartley)
Cockermouth, *Grey Goat* (Jennings)
Huntsman (Jennings)
Great Broughton, *Punch Bowl* (Jennings)
Hawkshead, *Outgate Inn* (Hartley)
High Lorton, *Horse Shoe* (Jennings)
Kendal, *Globe* (Yates and Jackson)
Keswick, *Woolpack* (Cumbria Brewers)
Milnthorpe, *Cross Keys* (Hartley)
Monkhill, *Drover's Rest* (Jennings)
Threlkeld, *Horse & Farrier* (Jennings)
Torpenhow, *Sun* (Jennings)
Ulverston, *Old Friends* (Hartley)
Rose & Crown (Hartley)
Workington, *Royal Oak* (Cumbria Brewers)

Isle of Man

Castletown, *Glue Pot* (Okell)
Union (Castletown)
Foxdale, *Foxdale* (Castletown)
Port Erin, *Falcon's Nest* (Okell)

YORKSHIRE AND THE NORTH-EAST

Brewers

Cameron, Hartlepool
Darley, Thorne
Hull Brewery, Hull
Northern Clubs Federation, Newcastle
Selby Brewery, Selby
Samuel Smith, Tadcaster
Timothy Taylor, Keighley
Theakston, Masham
Ward, Sheffield

Pubs

West Yorkshire

Addingham, *Fleece* (Tetley)
Bramhope, *Fox and Hounds* (Tetley)

Halifax, *Railway Inn* (Whitbread)
Haworth, *Royal Oak* (Webster)
Hebden Bridge, *Fox and Goose* (Whitbread)
Keighley, *Globe* (Taylor)
Volunteer (Taylor)
Kirkburton, *Woodman* (Taylor)
Leeds, *Old Unicorn* (Younger's)
Meltham, *Traveller's Rest* (Tetley)
New Mill, *White Hart* (Webster, Tetley)
Oxenhope, *Bay Horse* (Whitbread)
Pudsey, *Park* (Webster)
Stanbury, *Friendly* (Bass)
Wakefield, *Black Rock* (Tetley)

South Yorkshire

Sheffield, *Pomona* (Home)

North Yorkshire

Allerston, *Caylez Arms* (Cameron)
Appletreewick, *Craven Arms* (Theakston)
Arkengarthdale, *C.B. Hotel* (Theakston)
Asenby, *Shoulder of Mutton* (Whitbread, Younger's)
Bedale, *Oddfellows' Arms* (Theakston)
Brompton, *Black Swan* (Theakston)
Buckden, *Buck Inn* (Theakston)
Busby Stoop, *Busby Stoop* (Theakston)
Carlton Husthwaite, *Carlton Inn* (Theakston)
Catterick, *Bay Horse* (Theakston)
Chapel le Dale, *Hill Inn* (Theakston)
Cononley, *New Inn* (Taylor)
Copt Hewick, *Oak Tree Inn* (Theakston)
Easingwold, *George* (Cameron)
East Layton, *Foxhall Inn* (Theakston)
East Marton, *Cross Keys* (Theakston)
Exelby, *Green Dragon* (Webster, Theakston)
Fearby, *Black Swan* (Theakston)
Goathland, *Goathland Hotel* (Cameron)
Grassington, *Black Horse* (Theakston)
Forester's Arms (Tetley)
Grewelthorpe, *Hackfall Inn* (Theakston)
Hackness, *Hackness Grange* (Theakston)
Harome, *Star Inn* (Theakston)

Hawes, *Crown Hotel* (Theakston)
Helmsley, *Black Swan* (Younger's)
   Feathers (Younger's)
Hovingham, *Worsley Arms* (Younger's)
Huby, *New Inn* (Younger's)
Hutton Sessay, *Horsebreaker's Arms* (Younger's)
Ingleton, *Ingleborough* (Yates and Jackson)
   Three Horseshoes (Yates and Jackson)
Kettlewell, *Bluebell* (Theakston)
Kilburn, *Forester's Arms* (Tetley, Younger's)
Kirkby Malzeard, *Henry Jenkins* (Younger's)
Lastingham, *Blacksmith's Arms* (Theakston)
Malton, *Royal Oak* (Cameron)
Marton cum Grafton, *Punch Bowl* (Theakston)
Masham, *King's Head* (Theakston)
   White Bear (Theakston)
Middleham, *Black Swan* (Theakston)
Morton on Swale, *Non Plus Inn* (Theakston)
Northallerton, *Fleece* (Theakston)
   Porch House (Theakston)
Nosterfield (North Riding) *Freemason's Arms* (Theakston)
Pateley Bridge, *Watermill* (Theakston)
Richmond, *Bishop Blaize* (Cameron)
   Holy Hill Inn (Theakston)
Ripon, *Black Bull* (Theakston)
   Drovers (Theakston)
   Magdalen Inn (Theakston)
Rosedale Abbey, *Milburn Arms* (Cameron)
Sandsend, *Hart* (Cameron)
Scarborough, *Angel* (Cameron)
Scorton, *White Heifer Inn* (Theakston)
Scawton, *Hare* (Whitbread, Theakston)
Sherriff Hutton, *Old Highwayman* (Theakston)
Skipton, *Red Lion* (Whitbread)
Sutton, *Whitestone Cliff* (Younger's)
Sutton on Derwent, *St Vincent's Arms* (Theakston)
Thirn, *Boot and Shoe* (Theakston)
Thornton le Moor, *Black Swan* (Younger's)
West Tanfield, *Bruce Arms* (Theakston, Younger's)

Wighill, *White Swan* (Theakston)
Wykeham, *Downe Arms* (Younger's)
Yafforth, *Revellers* (Bass)
York, *Cross Keys* (Bass)

Cleveland

Guisborough, *Anchor Inn* (Theakston)
Marske by the Sea, *Clarendon* (Theakston)
Moorsholm, *Jolly Sailors* (Younger's)

Humberside

Beverley, *King's Head* (Hull)
Goole, *Cape of Good Hope* (Darley)
   Railway Inn (Hull)
Heck, *Bay Horse* (Theakston)
Howden, *Board* (Selby)

Tyne and Wear

Houghton Le Spring, *Oddfellows' Arms* (Vaux)
South Shields, *Adam and Eve* (Sam Smith)
Tynemouth, *Salutation* (Whitbread)

Durham

Pelton, *Bird* (Vaux)

Northumberland

Berwick on Tweed, *King's Arms* (Belhaven)
Belford, *Black Swan* (Vaux)
Blyth, *Waterloo* (Vaux)
Hexham, *Criterion* (Cameron)
Netherton, *Star* (Whitbread)

SCOTLAND

BREWERS

Belhaven, Dunbar
Maclay & Co., Alloa
Scottish and Newcastle, Edinburgh
Thomas Usher, Edinburgh
Traquair House, Innerleithen

PUBS

Borders

Innerleithen, *Traquair House* (Traquair House)

Central

Alloa, *Thistle Bar* (Maclay)
Alva, *Cross Keys Inn* (Maclay)
Clackmannan, *County* (Maclay)
Denny, *Royal Oak* (Belhaven)
Falkirk, *Woodside Hotel* (Belhaven)
Menstrie, *Hollytree* (Maclay)

Fife

Aberdour, *Forester's Arms*
   (Maclay)
Dunfermline, *Dander Inn*
   (Belhaven)
   Old Abbey Tavern (Belhaven)
Kincardine, *Bridge Bar* (Maclay)
Lochgelly, *Central Bar* (Belhaven)

Grampian

Aberdeen, *Dutch Mill Hotel*
   (Belhaven)

Lothian

Balerno, *Old Grey Horse*
   (Belhaven)
Belhaven, *Mason's Arms*
   (Belhaven)
Dunbar, *Eagle* (Belhaven)
   West Barns Inn (Belhaven)
Edinburgh, *Bennet's Bar*
   (Belhaven)
   Braid Hills Hotel (Belhaven)
Eskbank, *Justinless Inn* (Belhaven)
Penicuik, *Howgate Inn* (Belhaven)
Piershill, *Porter's Bar* (Belhaven)
Whitburn, *Cross Tavern*
   (Belhaven)

Strathclyde

Bishopton, *Golf Inn* (Belhaven)
Caldercruix, *Railway Tavern*
   (Belhaven)
Cambuslang, *Sefton Bar*
   (Belhaven)
   Toll Bar (Belhaven)
Coatbridge, *Forge Inn* (Maclay)
Dalmellington, *Snug Bar* (Maclay)
Glasgow, *Auld Hoose* (Belhaven)
Harthill, *Royal Bar* (Belhaven)
Johnstone, *Stand Bar* (Maclay)
Lanark, *Port Vaults* (Belhaven)
Strathaven, *Drumclog Inn*
   (Belhaven)
Uddingston, *Rowantree Inn*
   (Maclay)

Tayside

Alyth, *William Barnes* (Belhaven)
Arbroath, *Foundry Bar* (Belhaven)
   St Thomas Bar (Maclay)

Dundee, *Ascot Bar* (Belhaven)
   Bowbridge Bar (Belhaven)
Kinesswood, *Lomond Hotel*
   (Belhaven)

THE MIDLANDS

BREWERS

Allied Breweries, Burton on Trent
Batham, Brierley Hill
Davenport, Birmingham
Everards, Leicester
Hardy & Hanson, Kimberley,
   Notts.
Home Brewery, Daybrook, Notts.
Hoskins, Leicester
JPS, Brierley Hill
Mansfield Brewery, Mansfield
Marston, Burton on Trent
Ruddle, Oakham
Shipstone, Nottingham
Wolverhampton & Dudley
   Brewery

PUBS

Warwickshire

Fiveways, *Case Is Altered* (Ansell)
Henley in Arden, *Three Tuns*
   (Ansell)
Kenilworth, *Virgin and Castle*
   (Davenport)
Leamington, *Coach and Horses*
   (Davenport)
   Hope Tavern (Davenport)
   Red House (Mitchells and
   Butlers)
Napton, *Napton Bridge*
   (Davenport)
Stratford-on-Avon, *Shakespeare
   Hotel* (Donnington)
Warwick, *Red Lion* (Davenport)
   Woodman (Davenport)
   Zetland Arms (Davenport)

Staffordshire

Amington, *Gate* (Marston)
Burton on Trent, *Albion* (Marston)
   Blue Post (Bass Worthington)
   Victoria (Marston)
Cannock, *White Hart* (Banks)
Dunston, *Garth* (Banks)
Kinver, *Cross* (Hardy and Hanson)
   Elm Tree (Davenport)
   Olde Plough (JPS)
   Plough and Harrow (Batham)
   Ye Old White Hart (Hardy &
   Hanson)
Lichfield, *Angel* (Banks)
Shenstone, *Railway* (Marston)

Leicestershire

Barrow on Soar, *Navigation Inn* (Shipstone)
Billesdon, *Queen's Head* (Ruddle's)
Bisbrooke, *Gate* (Ruddle's)
Cottesmore, *Sun Inn* (Ruddle's)
Illston on the Hill, *Fox and Goose* (Ruddle's)
Langham, *Noel Arms* (Ruddle's)
Leicester, *Craddock* (Everard)
 Fosse Way (Marston)
 Shakespeare (Everard)
Loughborough, *Albion* (Shipstone)
 Blacksmith's Arms (Home)
 Gallant Knight (Everard)
 Griffin (Marston)
Market Bosworth, *Red Lion* (Hoskins)
Market Harborough, *Harborough Lounge* (Davenport)
 Cherry Tree (Everard)
Market Overton, *Black Bull* (Ruddle)
Medbourne, *Neville Arms* (Marston)
Melton Mowbray, *Black Swan* (Home)
 Noel Arms (Ruddle's)
Redmile, *Windmill Inn* (Ruddle's)
Sewstern, *Blue Dog* (Ruddle's)
South Croxton, *Golden Fleece* (Ruddle's)
Syston, *Baker's Arms* (Shipstone)
Uppingham, *Exeter Arms* (Ruddle's)
 Crown (Ruddle's)
Whissendine, *White Lion* (Ruddle's)

Derbyshire

Ashbourne, *Green Man and Black's Head* (Greenall Whitley)
Brassington, *Gate* (Marston)
Buxton, *Grone* (Robinson)
Crich, *Black Swan* (Hardy & Hanson)
 Cliff (Hardy & Hanson)
Ilkeston, *Durham Ox* (Ward)
 Horse & Groom (Shipstone)
Shardlow, *Dog and Duck* (Marston)
Willington, *Rising Sun* (Marston)

Nottinghamshire

Basford, *Barley Mow* (Home)
Burton Joyce, *Lord Nelson* (Shipstone)
Eastwood, *Sun* (Hardy & Hanson)

Mansfield, *King's Arms* (Mansfield)
 Old Ramme (Mansfield)
Sutton in Ashfield, *Duke of Sussex* (Hardy & Hanson)

West Midlands

Bilston, *Horse and Jockey* (Hanson)
Brierley Hill, *Holly Bush* (Batham)
 New Inn (JPS)
 Vine (Batham)
Brownhills, *Chase* (Banks)
Dudley, *White Swan* (Old Swan Brewery)
Greensforge, *Navigation* (JPS)
Netherton, *Old Swan* (Old Swan Brewery)
Shirt Heath, *United Kingdom* (Hanson)
Solihull, *Boat* (Davenport)
Stuckley, *Three Horseshoes* (Davenport)
Sutton Coldfield, *White Horse* (Davenport)

EAST ANGLIA

BREWERS

Adnams, Southwold, Suffolk
George Bateman, Wainfleet, Lincolnshire
Elgood, Wisbech, Lincolnshire
Greene King, Bury St Edmunds, Suffolk
Paine, St Neots, Cambridgeshire
Tollemache & Cobbold, Ipswich, Suffolk

PUBS

Norfolk

Aylsham, *Buckinghamshire Arms* (Adnams)
Blakeney, *Manor* (Adnams)
Blickling, *Buckinghamshire Arms* (Greene King)
Burnham Thorpe, *Lord Nelson* (Greene King)
Castle Acre, *Ostrich* (Greene King)
Clenchwarton, *Victory* (Elgood)
Downham Market, *Crown* (Worthington)
Gayton, *Crown* (Greene King)
Geldeston, *Wherry* (Adnams)
Harleston, *Cherry Tree* (Adnams)
Norwich, *Wild Man* (Tolly Cobbold)
Outwell, *Red Lion* (Elgood)

Weybourne, *Maltings* (Adnams)
Wiggenhall St Germain, *Crown &
Anchor* (Greene King)

Suffolk

Aldeburgh, *Black Horse* (Adnams)
   Mill (Adnams)
   White Hart (Adnams)
Badingham, *White Horse*
   (Adnams)
Beccles, *Loaves & Fishes* (Greene
   King)
Blyford, *Queen's Head* (Adnams)
Blythburgh, *White Hart* (Adnams)
Bramfield, *Bell* (Adnams)
Bungay, *Fleece* (Adnams)
Bury St Edmunds, *Falcon* (Greene
   King)
   Fox (Greene King)
   Greyhound (Greene King)
   Nutshell (Greene King)
   White Horse (Greene King)
Dennington, *Bell* (Adnams)
Felixstowe, *Little Ships* (Adnams)
Framlingham, *Railway Inn*
   (Adnams)
Halesworth, *Angel* (Adnams)
Ipswich, *Greyhound* (Adnams)
Kelsale, *Eight Bells* (Adnams)
   New Inn (Adnams)
   Rising Sun (Adnams)
Kentford, *Cock* (Greene King)
Kersey, *White Horse* (Adnams)
Leiston, *Engineer's Arms* (Adnams)
Long Melford, *Crown* (Adnams)
   Swan (Greene King)
Middleton, *Bell* (Adnams)
Newmarket, *Bull Hotel* (Greene
   King)
   White Lion (Greene King)
Orford, *Jolly Sailor* (Adnams)
   King's Head (Adnams)
Peasenhall, *Swan* (Tolly Cobbold)
Pin Mill, *Butt & Oyster* (Tolly
   Cobbold)
Rumburgh, *Buck* (Adnams)
Saxtead, *Marlborough Head*
   (Adnams)
Shadingfield, *Fox* (Adnams)
Sizewell, *Vulcan* (Adnams)
Snape, *Crown* (Adnams)
   Golden Key (Adnams)
Sotterley, *Falcon* (Adnams)
St James South Elmham, *White
Horse* (Adnams)
Southwold, *Crown* (Adnams)
   Lord Nelson (Adnams)
   Swan (Adnams)
Walberswick, *Anchor* (Adnams)
   Bell (Adnams)

Wangford, *Plough* (Adnams)
Wickham Market, *White Hart*
   (Adnams)
Wrentham, *Horse and Groom*
   (Adnams)
   Spread Eagle (Adnams)
Yoxford, *Blois Arms* (Adnams)

Cambridgeshire

Brampton, *Brampton Hotel*
   (Paine)
Bolnhurst, *Ye Olde Plough* (Paine)
Buckden, *Falcon* (Wells)
   Spread Eagle (Wells)
Cambridge, *Ancient Druids*
   (Wells)
   Elm Tree (Wells)
   Mill (Tolly Cobbold)
Gamlingay, *Cock* (Greene King)
Guyhirn, *Black Hart* (Elgood)
   Railway (Elgood)
Hail Weston, *Crown Inn* (Wells)
Harlton, *Hare and Hounds*
   (Wells)
Haslingfield, *Jolly Butchers* (Wells)
Huntingdon, *Victoria Inn* (Paine)
Kimbolton, *New Sun Inn* (Paine)
March, *Coachmaker's Arms*
   (Greene King)
   Horse and Jockey (Greene King)
   Jack of Trumps (Greene King)
   Prince of Wales (Greene King)
   Ship (Greene King)
Offord Cluney, *Swan Inn* (Wells)
Peterborough, *Royal Arms*
   (Elgood)
   Engine and Tender (Paine)
St Neots, *Greenacres* (Ruddle's)
   Golden Ball (Wells)
   Royal Oak (Paine)
Thorney, *Black Horse* (Elgood)
Upper Dean, *Three Compasses*
   (Wells)
Whaddon Gap, *Waggon & Horses*
   (Wells)
Wisbech, *King's Head* (Elgood)

Lincolnshire

Alford, *Half Moon* (Bateman)
Barnack, *Millstone Inn* (Ruddle's)
Bourne, *Golden Lion* (Sam Smith)
Edenham, *Five Bells* (Sam Smith)
Holbeach, *Bell* (Elgood)
Irnham, *Griffin* (Ruddle's)
Lincoln, *Roebuck* (Shipstone)
Little Bytham, *Willoughby Arms*
   (Ruddle's)
Louth, *Thatch* (Bateman)
Morton, *King's Head* (Ruddle's)

Navenby, *King's Head* (Sam Smith)
Old Somerby, *Fox & Hounds* (Ruddle's)
Stamford, *Dolphin* (Ruddle's)
  Golden Fleece (Ruddle's)
  Hurdler Inn (Ruddle's)
  Reindeer (Ruddle's)
Sutton Bridge, *Peacock* (Elgood)

HOME COUNTIES NORTH

BREWERS

Greene King & Sons, Biggleswade, Beds.
Charles Wells, Bedford, Beds.
Litchborough Brewing Co., Litchborough, Northants.

PUBS

Bedfordshire

Arlesley, *Steam Engine* (Wells)
Bolnhurst, *Ye Olde Plough* (Paine)
Clapham, *Fox & Hounds* (Wells)
Clophill, *Rising Sun* (Greene King)
Cotton End, *Harrows* (Wells)
Elstow, *Bull* (Greene King)
  Three Cups (Greene King)
Keysoe, *White Horse* (Wells)
Lidlington, *Green Man* (Greene King)
  Royal Oak (Wells)
Luton, *Bedfordshire Yeoman* (Greene King)
  Compasses (Wells)
  Fox (Greene King)
  George II (Greene King)
  White Lion (Wells)
Meppershall, *Airman* (Wells)
Millbrook, *Chequers* (Wells)
Old Warden, *Hare & Hounds* (Wells)
Potsgrove, *Fox & Hounds* (Wells)
Potton, *Red Lion* (Wells)
Renhold, *Polehill Arms* (Greene King)
Salford, *Red Lion* (Wells)
Sharnbrook, *Half Moon* (Wells)
  Swan with Two Necks (Wells)
Shefford, *Black Swan* (Wells)

Sutton, *John O'Gaunt* (Greene King)
Tebworth, *Queen's Head* (Wells)
Thurleigh, *Simple Jackal* (Wells)
Toddington, *Bedford Arms* (Wells)
  Nag's Head (Wells)
  Sow & Pigs (Greene King)
Turvey, *Three Cranes* (Paine)
Westoning, *Bell* (Greene King)

Buckinghamshire

Bow Brickhill, *Wheatsheaf* (Wells)
Cadmore End, *Ship* (Henley)
Chedington, *Rosebery Arms* (Wells)
Chenies, *Bedford Arms* (Younger's)
Frieth, *Prince Albert* (Henley)
Gayhurst, *Sir Francis Drake* (Wells)
Great Brickhill, *Duncombe Arms* (Wells)
Hanslope, *Watts Arms* (Wells)
High Wycombe, *Wendover Arms* (Henley)
Lavendon, *Horseshoe* (Wells)
Marlow, *Clayton Arms* (Henley)
Mentmore, *Stag Inn* (Wells)
Padbury, *Robin Hood* (Wells)
Simpson, *Plough* (Wells)
Skirmett, *Old Crown* (Henley)
Stoke Goldington, *White Hart* (Wells)
Wavendon, *Leathern Bottle* (Wells)

Northamptonshire

Ashton, *Crown* (Wells)
Blakesley, *Red Lion* (Litchborough)
Brixworth, *George* (Wells)
Duddington, *Royal Oak* (Ruddle's)
Farthingstone, *Pirate's Den* (Litchborough)
Grendon, *Half Moon* (Wells)
Little Harrowden, *Ten O'Clock* (Wells)
Maidford, *George* (Litchborough)
Mears Ashby, *Griffin's Head* (Wells)
Stoke Bruerne, *Boat* (M & B)
Stoke Doyle, *Shuckburgh Arms* (Ruddle's)
Towcester, *Saracen's Head* (Wells)
Yardley Hastings, *Red Lion* (Wells)